Scientific and Esoteric Encyclopedia of UFOs, Aliens and Extraterrestrial Gods

"A": Volume I from a set of 20 volumes.

*** *** ***

Maximillien de Lafayette

Volume I

SCIENTIFIC AND ESOTERIC ENCYCLOPEDIA OF UFOS, ALIENS AND EXTRATERRESTRIAL GODS

The world's first and most authoritative encyclopedia of its kind!!

Published in the United States of America and Germany.

Printed by Times Square Press. New York.
Date of Publication: July 22, 2014.

Scientific and Esoteric Encyclopedia of UFOs, Aliens and Extraterrestrial Gods

Volume I "A" from a set of 20 volumes.

Maximillien de Lafayette

***   ***   ***

Times Square Press
New York   Berlin   Paris   Madrid
2014

Table Of Contents

- Absu "Abzu", "Ab-su"
- "Apsû"
- Abulafia, Avraham ben Shmuel
- ACAMSD
- Accretion
- ACOM
- Adaam
- Adad
- Adad, Baal Cycle, and Yahweh fighting the dragon
- The Cycle of Baal
- Adama "Adamah"
- Adamu "Adapa"
- Adat "Adatt"
- Addu "Addur", "Addursham"
- Adon "Adonis"
- Adan, Jannat
- Adm
- Advanced quantum/relativity propulsion workshop, 1994
- Aerobiology
- Aerial Phenomena Group
- Aerial Phenomena Research Organization (APRO)
- Aerospace Defense Command (ADC)
- Aetherius Society
- AFL 202-2
- AFOSR
- Afqa "Afka"
- Afrit
- Agirim
- Agra-bida
- Agra-rihal
- Agusi
- Ahat "Aqhat"
- Ain
- Airship Flap of the 1896-1897 UFOs' sightings
- Different shapes of flying objects
- Ufologists' false claims, accounts and explanations
- Several types of crafts were built in Europe
- Several types of airships were built in the United States

11

- Headband Mental Command Device
- A new spaceship is built
- December 17 of 1923: A new model of the super Aldebaran's Jenseitsflugmaschine came to life
- January, 1924: The first successful flight of Adelbaran's Jenseitsflugmaschine
- Secretly manufacturing two small flying machines
- Maria Orsic's new two circular crafts

*** *** ***

A

A-dril "Adril": Name of a Gray-intraterrestrial hybrid alien, who according to governmemt's top secret files on aliens, a UFO's crash in Mexico, and alien abduction, worked on alien technology reverse engineering, the VT and BCB weapon systems at AUTEC and Area 51.

A-dril "Adril" was the center of a Pentagon's investigation of a UFO's crash in Mexico, which contained mutilated and burned parts of human bodies'

The investigation also encompassed discoveries of man-made UFOs, aliens living here on Earth, and an avalanche of top secret anti-gravity spacecrafts, known only to the Pentagon.

Was the UFO that crashed in Mexico of a German origin?

The answer is found in the interrogation of an alien hybrid by a 2 star General at The Pentagon. A senior civilian expert attended the interrogation. Before the hybrid-alien was brought in, the General asked the expert a few questions about the creature.

It went like that:

General: Sorry..., I have to talk to you about this, before we go to the meeting. Sit for a second, please. I received a very disturbing report from the Joint Chief of Staff.

I want your honest opinion, since you have mentioned The Black Shadows S-14, and alien abduction. Am not sure what to believe or who to believe, anymore. I want to settle this matter before the meeting. Look at this photograph. Do you know recognize this man?

Expert: AH Type 3.

General: Correct. Hybrid Alien Type 3.His name is Adril. He works for the CIA at Area 51.I am going to bring him here. He's next room. I want you to listen to him very carefully and tell me what you thing. Don't say a word to him. Just listen. OK?

Expert: General, he doesn't work for the CIA. He works for the Air Force. All AH Type 3 work for the Air Force.
General: You are absolutely sure?
Expert: Yes, General.

The Pentagon's Interview with hybrid A-dril.
General...on the phone: Bring him in.
Two guards bring Adril to the room.
General: Have a seat Adril. You still work at Area 51?
Adril: Yes, General.
General: What do you do there?
Adril: Propulsion and reverse-engineering.
General: Where did you work before?
Adril: Holloman, New Mexico. (Holloman Air Force Base, South of Alamogordo, New Mexico).
General: And before that?
Adril: Wright-Patterson, Ohio (Wright-Patterson Air Force Base, Fairborn, Ohio), Kirtland, New Mexico (Kirtland, Air Force Base, Albuquerque, New Mexico).
General: Didn't you work also at Andrews, Edwards and Los Alamos?
Adril: For a very short time.
General: What did you do there?
Adril: Reverse-engineering
General: Adril, we have a big problem with your people.
I am not very happy with Colonel... ...report. Tell me this...are you still working for the CIA and the Air Force?
Adril: No. For General... ..., and sometime at AUTEC.
General: What are you doing at AUTEC?
Adril: I am working on the VT and BCB.
General: The Vortex Tunnel and the Black Conic Box.
Adril: Yes, General.
General: Adril, we found human bodies' parts inside one of your crafts...You know, the one which crashed in Mexico, two weeks ago. And they were Americans!!
Adril: It wasn't our craft, General.
And they were native Mexicans from the Aztec's region, not Americans.

General: You're lying.

Adril: I am not lying. Why don't you check with AUTEC and the Air Force?

General: Whose craft was it then? You can't fool me Adril. It's not ours, for sure. I bet on it! It was one of your updated version Blue Fog T85s. Only you fly those spacecrafts.

Adril: The... ...too, fly the T85 and the T85D. You know very well General, the first and second models of T85 and Black Shadows S-14 are flown by the... ... and the... ... The reactor of the craft that crashed, uses QE, the Quadron Element. Ours use the CW and Plasma AGP (Plasma Anti Gravity Propulsion). And there is a big difference between the two.

Check your catalogue. See Specs... ... ...

General: We found 2 head-bands inside the craft! Your bands, damned! The bands you use for communication and underwater navigation. I know all about it. You attach them to your forehead to fly the craft. We don't have head-bands in our inventory.

Adril: The... ...have head-bands too, General!

General: Adril, abducting people is inadmissible! This is a big problem for us!! We have to stop this. And right now. You promised us no more abductions. What are you anyway? Ardi-Nishtaar? Hybrid? Aren't you also half human? Don't you feel anything for the abductees?

Adril: We are not abducting anybody, General. All abductions stopped 9 months ago. Somebody else is doing it, not us.

General: Who? Tell me who?

Adril: If not the..., then somebody else from another dimension. Admiral... ... knows all about it.

General: Then, you have to do something about it.

Adril: We can't. There is nothing we can do, General.

They are time machines, difficult to spot, impossible to chase.

General: Can't you shoot those bastards?

Adril: No general.

General (Looking at the civilian expert): I know somebody who can. OK, you can go. Hold on.

The General buzzes security. Two guards enter the room, and they escort Adril out.

General: What do you think ...(Talking to the civilian expert)?

Expert: He is lying through his teeth.
General: What makes you say that?
Expert: His neck was puffing. That's what happens when hybrids lie.
General: Bastards!

A-F1-XF (The Black Operations File):
I. Definition: A top secret file containing the most sensitive and controversial data and findings summaries of black operations and programs developed and executed by governmental agencies and the military, covering a multitude of projects and experiments. In addition to the US Air Force, only two agencies had access to this file.

II. Claims and conspiracy theories: Numerous ufologists and conspiracy theories advocates claim that abductions were part of sinister/experimental programs, and "Black Projects", carried on by the United States and aliens.
These frightening projects include:
  1- The development of highly sophisticated weapons systems,
  2- Exotic aircrafts,
  3- Psychological warfare,
  4- Mind control.
There are over 50 secret programs according to whistleblowers, and even the President of the United States is not fully informed about what is going on, said a military scientist, who allegedly has worked at S-41, Area 51, and Dulce Base.

III. The most known programs/projects are (to name a few):
1-Project Snowbird: Began in 1972.
Objectives: The development and technical research of the most sophisticated secret military spaceships based upon alien technology reverse engineering.
Agency or authority: Air Force, NASA and the CIA.
2-Project Aurora: Began in 1987.

16

Objectives: The design and building of the triangular-shaped spacecraft; a super hypersonic stealth aircraft that can exceed Mach 11.

c-Authority or agency: Air Force.

3-Project Excalibur:

Objectives: Exploring the possibility and the establishment of weapons systems to counter-attack aliens' invasions. This includes the development of technology capable of destroying all existing alien bases on earth, and especially the extraterrestrials underground and underwater bases.

Authority or agency: DOE, NSA, CIA and Air Force.

See Project Excalibur.

4-Project Blue Team: Merged with Sign Project.

Objectives: The recovery of crashed alien crafts.

Agency or authority: Air Force.

5-Project Sign: Changed to Grudge. Began in 1947.

Objectives: The evaluation of extraterrestrial threat to national security.

Agency or authority: Air Force, NSA, and the CIA.

6-Project Red Light: It was absorbed by Snowbird Project. Began in 1947.

Objectives: The cover-up of UFOs' sightings.

Agency or authority: Air Force.

7-Project Grudge/Aquarius: Began in 1949. It was absorbed by Blue Book.

Objectives: To retrieve, collect and assess UFOs' sightings, alien cultures, extraterrestrial technology, contacts with alien life forms, including all the technological, scientific, medi
cal and intelligence information pertaining to these fields.

Agency or authority: NASA, CIA, NSA, and Air Force.

8-Project Moon Dust and Blue Fly:

Objectives: The investigation and analyses of the most documented and reliable UFOs' sightings, photos, and witnesses' reports, including retrieving UFOs' crashes.

Agency or authority: Air Force and the CIA.

9-Project Blue Book: Began in 1952 and ended in 1969.

Objectives: Putting an end to all the UFOs sightings reports.

Agency or authority: Air Force and the CIA.

17

10-Project Magnet: Began in 1950 in collaboration with the Canadian Air Force.
Objectives: The test-fly of recovered UFOs.
Authority or agency: Air Force (US and Canada).
11-Project Pounce/Pluto:
Objectives: Study and evaluation of alien technology and its implications in military sciences.
Authority or agency: NSA, CIA and Air Force.
12-Project Gabriel/Joshua: Began in 1972.
Objectives: The development of a super, low frequency pulsed sound system to destroy alien weapons.
Authority or agency: DOE, NSA, CIA and Air Force.
13-Project Plato:
Objectives: Establishing and implementing a protocol for diplomatic representations and relations with extraterrestrials.
Authority or agency: The White House, NSA, CIA and Air Force.
14-Project Luna:
Objectives: The investigation and assessment of alien bases and underground facilities on the dark side of the Moon.
Authority or agency: NSA, NASA, CIA and Air Force.
15-Project Crystal Knight: The information came from sources connected to the British intelligence organization MI6.
Objectives/operation: It focuses on the experiences, and assessment of data/information of all those who were directly connected with aliens' projects following initial contacts with extraterrestrials in 1940s.
Authority or agency: U.S. Defense Intelligence Agency (DIA), NSA, and CIA.
16-Project SERPO: Whistleblowers and some military insiders claimed that a 12-person U.S. military team was sent to the home planet of visiting extraterrestrials during the 1960s and 70s.
The planned 10-year stay was a part of an exchange program and was reportedly called Project Crystal Knight, with the later code name Project SERPO after the team returned home.
Authority or agency: U.S. Defense Intelligence Agency (DIA), Air Force, and NASA.
17-TAC Star Project:

Objectives: Utilizing a newly created military communication system (TAC-STAR), the US Air Force and NASA were able to somehow (never understood how) wire in instructions to military spatial stations located beyond but nearby Earth's orbit, by using a TAC-STAR keyboard.

Mode of operation: This would enable the military and scientists to type English letters into the alien communication system. One military scientist said: "Our numbering system was similar to that of the aliens, and although our numerical designations were different, we were able to use lines, dots and numbers to indicate the corresponding number. After several exchanges of messages, the aliens got it before we got theirs. It was obvious to us that we were dealing with a highly advanced civilization...they did not send complete sentences, but they sent enough for us to understand the meaning of the message.

From that point on, we communicated only in English except for numbers. We grasped their numbering system pretty quickly and used their numbering system since we did not wish to provide them with wrong landing coordinates.

We eventually provided them with the latitude and longitude coordinates."

Authority or agency: U.S. Defense Intelligence Agency (DIA), United States Air Force, and NASA. See TAC Star Project.

18-D.A.R.P.A. (Defense Advanced Research) Project:

Nature/scope: Basically, it deals with the most sophisticated alien technology reverse engineering programs.

Authority or agency: CIA, NSA, U.S. Defense Intelligence Agency (DIA), United States Air Force, and NASA.

19-MK Ultra Mind Control Program: Self-explanatory.

Authority or agency: CIA.

A'Khalka: Ulemite/Anunnaki term for the creation of the first man on Eath.

Also known as Akalicha "Akalikha". It is composed of two words:

a-An, which means origin; god; beginning;

b-Kalicha, which means the Creation.

The Anunnaki's creation of the world was briefly described in the Sumerian texts; only one account of the Sumerian creation has survived, but it is a suggestive one.

The creation account appeared as an introduction to the story of the Huluppu-Tree.

The creation of Man by the Anunnaki: From the Mesopotamain cuneiform clay tablet:
Here is the translation of the original Sumerian texts:
Nintu and Enki plan the creation of the human race (I: 178-220);
Enki, rather than Anu, is speaking at this time.
In these versions, Enki reveals his plan for creating the human race. Enki said:
"While Nintu the birth-goddess is here,
let her create the offspring...
let man carry the basket of labor of the Anunna (gods)."

Enki and Nintu called the goddess and said to her:
"You are the goddess of birth
and the creator of man.
Create for the Gods, the Lulu (man),
Let him bear the yoke,
let Lulu carry the basket of labor
of the Anunna. "
Important note: The Anunnaki did not come to Earth to mine gold. The Sumero-Akkadian phrase on the Sumerian tablet: *"the labor-basket of the gods"* means that first humans were created to work the fields and feed the Anuna (Gods), fill up the basket of food, fruits and cereals, and not to mine for gold.

Geshtu-e: The slaughtered Igigi god and the creation of the "First Man": Geshtu-e is the Akkadian/Sumerian name of the Igigi god whose blood and intelligence were used by the Anunnaki Mami to create the first man.
In the beginning, before men were created, the Anunnaki, (the extraterrestrial gods living on planet Earth), had to till the land and water it to grow their food. And this was hard and extremely demanding labor.

Enlil summoned the Igigi, and asked them to do the job.

The Igigi's revolt:
In addition to cultivating and working the fields in ancient Iraq (Babylon, Sumer), Enlil assigned to the Igigi, the hard tasks of digging trenches, canals, and river beds.
And the Igigi kept on doing this hard labor for centuries, until they could not take it anymore. They threw down their tools and went en masse to Ekur, Enlil's citadel at Nippur, to protest this hardship, and to demand immediate relief.

When the Igigi reached the citadel, Enlil ordered Nusku, his doorkeeper, to keep them out of Ekur.
Nusku asked Enlil:
"Why do you fear your sons?
Call the other gods and let
them help solve this thing."

So Enlil summoned the gods, including Anu and Enki.
Together, they rushed to help Enlil, and stood firm on the ramparts of the citadel, and spoke to the furious Igigi:
"Why are you attacking us?
And the Igigi answered:
"The work you have assigned to us is killing us;
we can no longer bear it.
We have stopped digging the trenches
and we are declaring war."

Enki asked the gods for advice, and said to them:
"Why do we blame the Igigi?
Their tasks are too hard.
Goddess Mami is with us.
Let her create human beings to serve us
and to do the work of the Igigi.
So we can put the yoke
of Enlil on these creatures
and let the Igigi return to heaven."

21

The Anunnaki decided to create humans:
The gods agreed, and asked goddess Mami to create beings to do the work of the Igigi, not to mine for gold.
Mami said:
"It is not wise for me to do all this.
You should choose Enki instead,
because he is wise and does things right.
But if he prepares the clay needed
to complete the task,
I will create these beings."

Enki replied:
"If we use only clay to create new beings,
they will be like animals, without intelligence.
Instead, we must slaughter one of the gods,
to make these creatures capable
of bearing Enlil's yoke.
We can mix his flesh and blood
with clay to create a Man."

The Anunnaki seized Geshtu-e, and slaughtered him:
The Anunnaki seized Geshtu-e, the Igigi god of wisdom and knowledge, and slaughtered him. As soon as his flesh and blood were mixed with the clay, a Shabbah (Ghost) manifested, and took the shape of a human being.
Mami seized the ghost, and divided him into fourteen pieces, to create seven females and seven males. These creatures were the first prototypes of the human race.

Mami presented her creatures to the Anunnaki, and said:
"I have done everything you have asked.
I have created Man (Men and Women).
And I gave them the faculty of speaking,
so they could talk to each other
and do the job.
Let each Man choose a wife.
And Ishtar will bless them
with healthy children,

to fill the whole Earth
with generations of servants."

Note: This is why and how Man was created by the Anunnaki at that time in history. Humans were created to do the Igigi's hard labor in the fields, and to feed the Anunnaki. And not to mine gold as erroneously claimed by ancient astronauts and ancient aliens theorists, and famous authors in the West!!
The Mesopotamian tablets never, ever mentioned that the Anunnaki came to planet Earth to mine for gold, or they created humans to mine for gold either!
The Mesopotamian tablets made it clear to us that the Anunnaki created mankind to replace the Igigi who complained constantly because of the heavy agricultural work which included working the fields, digging waters' canals, irrigation, planting, harvesting, feeding the gods, and an avalanche of other hard physical works at Nippur, the Anunnaki imposed upon them for many years.

"A-TTT": An acronym for the "Tag Team Tunnel".
The American military has successfully sent six men through a vortex tunnel, sometimes jokingly referred to as "the straw".
This vortex tunnel can be turned on and turned off at will, and is a project that started in the 1960's and became fully operational in the 1970's. The Americans successfully sent some of its military personnel who volunteered for the experiment; they were sent through a vortex tunnel to another dimension and were brought back safely.
Within close circles, the Tag Team Tunnel is also referred to as the "TTT", or "A-TTT".
The team of six were sent through the vortex and were supposed to have returned within a matter of ten to fifteen seconds, but ended up gone for fifteen minutes.
When they asked the Gray who was working with them on this project why the men had not immediately returned, the Gray laughed at them, at which point they demanded he goes through the tunnel himself to retrieve the men.
Within a few seconds, all six men and the Gray were back.

In the debriefing that followed, the six volunteers said that the dimension they were in was so close to ours, as to be able to see and hear one Major put a gun to the head of the Gray, saying "You better go in there right now buddy and get my men back!"

The Gray laughed at him but eventually returned with the six.

Apparently all Gray aliens are known to play tricks and games like these with the military, within many of these joint projects.

What did the men see, hear and feel in this other dimension so close to ours?

According to the men, they saw a labyrinth of corridors before them, and the only colors they saw were blue; light blue and light gray. No other colors seemed to exist in this other dimension.

There was no sound or breeze or any kind, and they felt a void in the corridors. The only sounds they could hear were those of the military personnel, the Major in charge of the operation, and the cameramen behind them who were observing and filming this experiment.

Turning around to return to the room, the six volunteers said they encountered "the most unusual invisible, intangible wall which would not let them exist the dimension they entered."

When the Gray went in to retrieve the six men from that dimension, they observed a strange device on his wrist that he had withheld from the military; he used the device to "separate our physical world from a parallel dimension" in which we were trapped." Upon stepping in, he grabbed a hold of the first man, and placed his other hand up to the invisible intangible wall of that dimension.

The device on his wrist revealed a knob on the wall, which he turned from left to right, and then told the men they could move forward.

As the first man went through, to the second man standing right behind, it was as if he dematerialized to the width of a page in a book flipped over.

The wall of that dimension now became foggy, and the other men were terrified of going through it, not knowing whether they too would be turned into sheets of paper. The Gray assured the men it was perfectly safe, and going through the "foggy layer" was the only way to get out, so the men had no choice but to go through.

What are the military implications and applications of this technology?

Imagine being able to transport an enemy troops unit, or even an entire military base, to that parallel dimension. Within the void of that dimension, there would be no food, no water, no stimuli of any kind that the human body and mind is used to.

Whoever is sent there would go insane from sensory deprivation, whilst starving to death from hunger and thirst. This technology has reached the final stage of its development. Worth mentioning here that the Philadelphia Experiment was a precursor to this kind of vortex tunnel technology.

Mode of operation and purpose:

When activated (usually done in open fields in the American mid-west, away from farming and populated areas), an invisible vortex opening that is about ten foot wide, sucks in everything in its path, up to 500 feet in all directions. "This is only one of its functions. Its primary purpose is to do just the opposite..." said a well-informed insider. See Vortex Tunnel.

A1: Term for the first category of aliens (non-human species) as classified by the government, and mentioned in the secret "CAS" Catalogue of Aliens Species, compiled between 1948 and 1951 by the USAF. See aliens' categories

A2: Term for the second category of aliens (non-human species) as classified by the government, and mentioned in the secret "CAS" Catalogue of Aliens Species, compiled between 1948 and 1951 by the USAF. See aliens' categories

A3: Term for the third category of aliens (non-human species) as classified by the government, and mentioned in the secret "CAS" Catalogue of Aliens Species compiled between 1948 and 1951 by the USAF. See aliens' categories

Aa: Assyrian/Akkadian/Babylonian/Sumerian. Noun.

Aa, Ea.

The Babylonian, Sumerian and Assyrian deity often referred to as Aê, and Ea. He is also represented by and identified as Au, Ya'u /Ya which is a variation of Ea, an ancient Babylonian deity.
Ya corresponds to the Hebrew Au, Aw, Awu.
From Ya, the Hebrew words Yah or Jah derived, and were used as prefix for Yahweh.

Ea "Enki" stepping on a dry land, a gesture symbolizing his supreme authority over Earth. The dry-land as depicted in this cylinder refers also to ramparts protecting the cities of his kingdom. From the ramparts emerge a stream of fishes, symbol of all life-forms in the sea. Thus, his authority extends to dry lands and seas of the Earth.

Aa had numerous names and titles; he was the Babylonian and Assyrian god of water, rivers, the sea, the arts, and crafts.

He warned Pir-napistim of the Deluge, and instructed him to build a ship to save his family, himself, all the birds, and the animals of the earth.

Worth mentioning here that the Babylonian Pir-napistim became the Chaldean/Biblical Noah. See Pir-napistim, and Ya'u.

Sea Ea, and Enki.

Anunnaki God Ea accompanied by two deities in the form of a scorpion and a dragon.

A slab from Tell Asmar in Iraq, depicting the Anunnaki God Ea accompanied by two deities in the form of a scorpion and a dragon. The scorpion represented wisdom and determination, while the dragon represented authority and the primordial female aspect of the Creation.

Aakil: Name of the first Anunnaki leader to be called the "Fallen Commander", because he fell in love with the "Women of Earth". In religious scriptures, he is known as the "Fallen Angel."

Aakim-lu: "The female creator of the Anunnaki and the Igigi, and the seven galaxies" according to the Book of Ramadosh.
Aa-kim-lu used Rouh-D'ab-Sha.Lim to create the Anunnaki, some seven billions years ago. According to Ulema esoterism, the word Aa-lim-lu represents the Kadoushu (Sacred), and should be only used during extraterrestrial plasmic manifestations. Indeed, the Anunnaki revealed to the Munawariin "Enlightened Masters" that the world was created by a female energy (A woman life-form), and her creation included the Anunnaki and all the races that lived in the seven galaxies of light.
Aa-kim-lu's geometrical presentation or symbol is a spear with three bursting stars.
The tree stars represent the three separate ages of the universe.
It is very clear, that Madame Blavatsky's theory on the age of the universe as presented in her theosophical "Secret Doctrine" was directly influenced by the three stars of Aa-kim-lu.

Aamala: The Anunnaki's registry of future events. Aamala is used as a calendar to show important events that will occur on other planets. According to Ulema Rajani, time is not linear. And because space bends on itself, therefore, events don't have a chronology or time-sequences.
Things and events happen on the net of the cosmos, and when your mind perceives them, they happen before your eyes. In reality, they have already happened before you had the time and means to notice them. This applies to all future and forthcoming events, simply because they have occurred on another cosmos' net, which is parallel to another world which contains separate, yet identical events.
It is a matter of perception, rather than observation or taking notice..." said Anunnaki Ulema Govinda.

Aaska-az: Anunnaki/Hittite. Noun. A gate.

29

Helena Petrovna Blavatsky.

This word appeared in the language of the Hittite and Ana'kh, and meant gate in general. However, in Ana'kh, Aaska-az means the major gate of an Anunnaki colony established in Sumer and Phoenicia, particularly cities like Baalbeck and Nineveh.

Ab: The Anunnaki's lord who established the rules regulating and governing family's affairs. He is also referred to as the "Good father." However, Anunnaki women are in total charge of the daily affairs of the family, and are responsible for the education of their children. Despite the enormous power and authority of "Ab", the Anunnaki's society remains a matriarchal community. "The Anunnaki have families, fathers, mothers, and children too, and they follow familial hierarchy, as we do here on Earth..." said Anunnaki Ulema Najani.

Unlike other extraterrestrial races and species that are not built around family structure and parental bonds, the Anunnaki live within their own families' perimeter, and show feelings and emotional reactions as we do, said Anunnaki Ulema Al Bakr.

He added, "The head of a living unit or a family is the father.

However, the family is always placed under the direct guidance of a mother. Anunnaki society is matriarchal."

From the Anunnaki word "Ab", derived the Arabic word "Ab", which means father, and the Assyrian word "Ab", which is an abbreviation of Abu, Abi, Abim, meaning father.

It was mentioned in the ancient Mesopotamian and Assyrian clay tablets; "Abi alidi-ka", meaning "Of the father begetting thee."

When "i" is added to Ab, the meaning becomes: My father. This is quite common in many Semitic and ancient Middle and Near Eastern languages. For instance, Abi becomes "my father".

In the following Assyrian passages, the word Abi is clearly understood as my father.

"Itti sa abi ipusu" which means "What my father did."

"Sa Nabupalhuzur abi banu-a ipusu" means: Which Nabopalasar, my father begetting me, made.

Abba "Habba": Anunnaki/Assyrian. Noun. The sea.

Abba "Habba" appeared in Assyrian and Ana'kh languages.

The Annals of Sardanapalus contained the following relevant passage: "Istu ebirtan nahr Tiggar adi Libnana va habba rabte." It means: "From the passage of the river Tigris to Lebanon and the great sea." In Nebi Yunnus, Sennacherib said: "Sa ina ebirtan habba..." It means: "Which is the crossing of the sea."

31

In Ana'kh, Abba "Habba" was the first name given to the Mediterranean Sea by the Anunnaki.

Worth mentioning here that the Mediterranean Sea was a major source of natural resources sought by the Anunnaki. Among the Anunnaki's first colonies on Earth, were Arwad, Malta, Tyre (Modern day Sour), Sidon (Modern day Saida), Byblos (Modern day Jbeil), Afka and Batroun; all are located on the shores of Habba, the Mediterranean Sea.

The old city of Sidon.

Abd: Sumerian/Akkadian/Arabic/Babylonian. Noun.
Historically, Abd was the first name given to Man.
The original meaning was slave, but later on, Enki changed it to servant. In contemporary Arabic, it is written either as Abd or Abed and it means:
1-A black person.

2-A slave.

Many derogatory attributions for Abd are found in the Arabic poems of Abu Al Tiib Al Mutanabbi (915-65 A.D.), in the writings of Abu Al'Ala' Al'Maari (died in 1057), and Al-Nabigha Al-Zoubyani (535-604), and in the story of king Dabshalim and Brahman Baydaba. (Around 175 B.C.)

Abu Al Tiib Al Mutanabbi (915-65 A.D.)

Abductee: Any person who is believed or assumed to have been kidnapped, and/or taken aboard an alien craft without his or her consent. See Abduction, alien.

Abduction, alien: An abductee is usually any person who is believed or assumed to have been kidnapped, and/or taken aboard an alien craft without his or her consent. Abduction is the act or process of such kidnapping.

I. The reports and accounts of abductees; generalities:

It was reported by abductees that their abductors, the Grays, quite often, talk to them about the future of the human race, and Earth; a future based upon the creation and population of a new race, which shall live and prosper on Earth for a very long time.

And during this process, the human race will reach a higher level of awareness, intelligence, and science.

This higher level of knowledge at multiple levels is the result of the creation of a hybrid race, which is far superior to us. And by the end of that process, the human race will vanish from the face of the Earth.

However, there is a considerable number of abductees who told us that the Grays have no intention to destroy the human race.

On the contrary, they wish to live with us, here on Earth, in peace, harmony and share with us, their highly advanced science, knowledge and understanding of the universe.

This group of abductees also said that the Grays have a great affection toward us, and the babies they have genetically created using human DNA and Grays' genes are very dear to them, for they have called them, the children of the future; a future to be equally shared with the Grays.

In either case, the agenda of the Grays is clear: Using humans as a genetic source.

Abductees reports and accounts contain extensive and detailed stories about their contact with the Grays, their habitats, way of life, collective and personal relationships between abductees and aliens, nutrition system, activities, messages about the future of the human race and Earth, concerns and worries of the Grays, holographic projections of scenes and events pertaining to the history of the human race and our future, and an avalanche of fascinating information on multiple levels.

II. Abductions have ceased:

Abductions began years ago, but recent governments' secret reports have revealed without any doubt, that abductions have ceased some six years ago, because, finally, the Grays cracked down the secrets and codes of "DNA Reproduction Sequences", and the "Intra-Breeding Molecules Duplication," according to a governmental report.

Outsider scientists mocked the whole idea, and stated that the DNA Reproduction Sequences is a pure non-sense. But insiders disagree. They are absolutely sure that the Grays have found a way to save their "Doomed Race", and humans' abduction is no longer necessary. Ufologists are not convinced, and more books on current abductions are published every year by the dozens; some, are never read, others made waves on the landscape of ufology, and fueled debates on the Internet.

I am absolutely sure that abductions are no longer *en force*.III: The Grays and "Global Change".

The Grays told the abductees: The future will bring a "Global Change". What kind of future, the Grays are talking about? How do the Grays define a new future for humans? Are they Grays part of our future? Why and how?

Are we controlled by the Grays?

Are the Grays malevolent or benevolent?

These questions were asked by abductees, as well as by top echelon in the military, scientists and ethicists working for governments on projects/operations related to aliens, Grays, and abductions. The governments of Brazil, Mexico, Russia and the United States have elaborate files on these subjects.

Only insiders and some very privileged scientists have access to these files. But they are not talking. According to government's insiders, the Grays or intraterrestrials/extraterrestrials topics are Above Top Secret, and therefore, revealing/disclosing pertinent information will jeopardize national security. It is very possible, especially, if we take into consideration, the implication and effects, these information will have on the social structure of our society, religious beliefs, and protection of citizens.

In other words, the governments' files are sealed, and do not expect to learn anything about and from these files. Thankfully and fortunately, some abductees are talking.

Their accounts abound. Among the most critical issues, jointly discussed by the abductees and their abductors, the Grays, are:

- a-Earth's safety,
- b-The future of the human race.

IV: The future of the human race and the global change:
Abductees told us that the Grays will bring a global change to our societies, lives and future. It is a bright and very promising future, because the Grays are going to get rid of all of our social problems, such as greed, hunger, violence, illnesses, diseases, crimes, poverty, political ambitions, injustice, so on.

In addition, the Grays shall establish a new world order, based upon peace, prosperity and cosmic awareness.

By doing so, we will, for the first time ever, learn about the true history of mankind, our origin, why we are here, all the facts and lies written in our recorded history, our relationship to God, and the worlds and dimensions around us.

In numerous encounters with the aliens, the abductees witnessed extraordinary holographic projections of events from our history, past, present and future. For instance, the abductees told us that they saw on a very large screen, scenes from the destruction of planet Earth, assassinations, catastrophes, bloody events, and the murder of presidents, heads of states, prophets, and saints.

The Grays told the abductees, that all these horrifying events in the history of man, prevented us from:

- a-Reaching a higher level of intelligence,
- b-Understanding how the universe functions,
- c-Finding cures for our fatal diseases,
- d-Living in peace,
- e-Progressing in many/various fields, including science, medicine and technology.

The Grays also told the abductees, that they will bring a global change to our lives, by "prescribing a new future" for all of us.

This global change will alter everything we have believed in, especially religious dogmas, and the origin of mankind.

To do so, the Grays need the cooperation of the abductees.

What kind of cooperation, are they talking about? Why only the abductees are in a position to help the Grays, and not the rest of us? How long it would take the Grays to change our world, our societies, and our future?

How the grays will change our lives and future? Answers to some of these questions were provided in abductees' accounts. The Grays did not reveal everything to the abductees. The Grays' explanations rotated around the status quo of our social systems, the climate, environmental problems, and the safety of planet Earth. Basically, and essentially, the Grays fear that continuous detonations of nuclear bombs will eventually destroy Earth, which they have called their own habitat. The Grays are not going to allow such destruction, because they live here on Earth.

"They lived on the surface of Earth, underground and undersea, for millions of years, long before a human or a beast-human walked on the surface of the Earth..." told us Arlene S, an abductee who lived with the Grays in one of their habitats, for two months.

Arlene S. said that this is what the Grays told her, before they took her to a hybridization room, where they operated on her.

Abductees personal accounts:

a-The personal account of Manuel E. G., an abductee from Vera Cruz: Manuel E. G., told me (Verbatim, word for word and unedited):

Note: I had to use the dots "..." to hide the name and identity of people, Mr. E.G. has mentioned to me.

"I was taken inside a big UFO, a very big one, and the aliens showed me big cities in flames, burning forests, and armies shooting at people. Many many dead people everywhere. The UFO flew over Washington, DC, Arizona, Alaska, Mexico City, and cities in Russia. From the windows of the UFO, I saw very terrible things, bombs' explosions, a big flood and something like one half of the earth falling into a big hole, as if the Earth was cut into two pieces.

For a moment, I thought I was dreaming, but when I looked around me, I understood I am not dreaming. I knew I am awake and something very strange, very new is happening to me.

You must believe me I was not dreaming, because I saw many people inside the UFO and all of them were scared. Nobody said a word and they kept on looking from the windows. I am sure they saw everything I saw.

I should tell you I recognized some of the people who were inside the UFO. This is true. I saw... the Governor of..., he was there, he was there, I recognized his face, I know who he is, I saw him many times on television. In a seat behind him, I saw..., do you know who he is?

He is famous, many people watch his TV show, he was there. Next to him I saw Bishop...yes sir, Bishop...he was looking and looking outside, and his face was so closed to the window. I knew all these people.

Then I said to myself, this is something unbelievable. Nobody is going to believe me if I tell them what I saw. While I was talking to myself to understand what it is going on here, a short person who did not look like us walked around the seats of the UFO and began to talk to us. All of us turned our heads to listen to him.

At the very beginning he began to talk in a language I did not understand.

I know, I can tell you that, it was not Spanish or English. Some language I have never heard before. I think the other people too, did not understand what he was saying.But a few seconds later, this strange looking person begins to speak to us in English. He had a very strange accent, it was a good English but his accent was not American. But I understood what he was saying.

I don't remember everything he told us. But I remember what he told us about what we saw from the windows. He said we are looking at cities that people on Earth are going to destroy in the future. They are going to destroy Earth because they are violent. Wars will be everywhere on Earth, and millions will die.

While he was talking to us, the UFO made a sudden turn, very very fast, we felt this but we stayed in our seats, and nobody fell down, we had no seat belts and I could not understand why I did not fell down or did not hit the seat before me.

One second please, I must say something about this strange looking person. He is not a human being. He did not look like me or like you. He was short, less than five feet. The color of his face was light gray, not too much gray, but something like that, you know, a strange color that changed to a green gray, something like that.

He was wearing a uniform, a suit, it looked like aluminum, metallic, like a soft glass, and it shined sometimes like a mirror. I did not see any badge on his uniform. Nothing.

No pockets, no belts, no buttons, nothing, only a metallic suit from his neck to his feet.

I did not see shoes, nothing, one long suit, that' all. Okay?

Okay, after the UFO turned, the alien, can I say this, alien? I am sure he is alien, not human. Okay. The alien told us not to be afraid, and very soon, all of us we will return safe to our homes. Nothing bad is going to happen to us.

Then, the alien person told us to look from the window.

Everybody turned his head and started to look from the window. We saw buildings and hangars, antennas, towers and landing strips.

Yes, a few helicopters, soldiers and jeeps.

Now I remember, we saw also barbed wires and big fences, something like that. The alien said we are looking now at military bases in the United States.

He said, these bases have nuclear weapons, and they are the biggest danger for humans. The Earth will be destroyed by these bases. But his people are going to save us all.

He also said some bases have weapons systems that can change the climate and weather of Earth, and this is very dangerous because the whole Earth will be destroyed if its climate changes. There will be no more food, vegetables or anything to eat. People on Earth will not be able to see the Sun again.

We will die from a freezing weather. And the Earth will become a big desert covered with ice. But before that, the Earth will explode, all the forests will burn, a big flood will cover all the lands, no more mountains, no more buildings, no more stores, no more people, finish, this is the end of the world.

All the people inside the UFO were very afraid, and no one could say a word. Nothing. The alien was looking at us, and I felt that he was reading our minds.

Suddenly, his voice became more human.

I did not see him smiling. He never smiled. I did not know or understand how he was talking to us. His mouth never moved. His lips never moved.

His voice came from somewhere from inside his body. I did not know where from."
Interviewing Manuel E. G:
This was the verbal account of Manuel E. G., an abductee from Vera Cruz, Mexico. Later on, I asked him if this was everything he heard or saw. He replied: "Not really, I don't know, I don't remember, maybe, I don't know."
Question: "Did the alien tell you how he is going to change all this? Is he going to stop all wars on Earth?"
Manuel: Yes, he did. One second please. Okay, he said his people who live with us are going to make all the military bases disappear. Finish, no more bases for nuclear bombs.
Question: What do you mean by "people who live with us"?
Manuel: I don't know.
Question: Did he tell you how his people "are going to make all the military bases disappear?"
Manuel: Yes. He said, his people who love us very much and care for us, are going to change these bases into gardens. They will make big holes in the earth and bury the bases inside.
Question: Did he describe these holes?
Manuel: I don't remember.
Question: Did he tell you when his people are going to make these military bases disappear?
Manuel: I don't remember.
Question: Did the alien explain to all of you what he meant by "weapons systems that can change the climate and weather of Earth"?
Manuel: Maybe. I don't remember.
Question: How did you get home? Did the UFO return you to the place where you were takenn from, or.... (I was interrupted)
Manuel: I am not sure. I was driving my car, and suddenly I saw myself inside a UFO. When I returned, my car was still there, I start walking toward my car. I felt a little bit dizzy. You know, like a headache, I drove my car. I was a little bit tired and I could not understand what had happened to me.
I thought I was dreaming, or maybe going crazy.

And while driving I start to remember things. I said to myself I am not going to tell anybody about what I saw and what had happened to me. They will think I am crazy.
Question: Did you talk to anybody who was inside the UFO?
Manuel: No.
Question: Why not?
Manuel: Because I could not move.
I could not open my mouth.
Question: Did you feel paralyzed or maybe under the influence of some sort of hypnotism?
Manuel: I don't know.
I could listen, I could see lots of things, but I could not talk or move. Something was holding me in my seat.
Question: Can you describe your seat?
Manuel: My seat? Inside the UFO?
All the seats looked alike.
They are not like an airplane seats. They were round. They were not positioned in rows, you know, like seats in an airplane, one after another. They were positioned inside a large circle.
Question: So, how could you see what was going on outside the UFO, if the seats were positioned inside a circle?
Were the windows also positioned inside a circle?
Manuel: Correct.
Question: What do you mean?
Manuel: I mean the seats were next to windows, and everything, windows and seats were inside a circle. You look around you and you see windows next to seats and people sitting in their seats looking from the windows.
Question: How big were the windows?
Manuel: Not very big. They are round, small, and had no frame around them.
Question: What do you mean by "no frame around them"?
Manuel: Each window was joined to another window by a glass sheet. It appeared to me as if the windows were big dots inside a mirror or a fiberglass panel.
Question: How long did you stay inside the UFO?
Manuel: I don't remember.
Question: Do you remember when did you return to your car?

41

Manuel: No, I don't remember.

Question: Well, was it day or night? In the morning or in the afternoon?

Manuel: When I returned to my car it was around 5 o'clock, PM.

Question: Do you remember what did you see or hear before 5:00 PM?

Manuel: I was in my car, that' all, and when I returned to my car, it was 5:00 PM, maybe a little bit later, maybe 5:10, 5;20 or something like this. I don't remember what happened to me when I was taken from my car.

Question: Do you remember the time when you were taken from you car?

Manuel: Let me see. Maybe 4:30 or 4:50, I am not sure.

Question: So, you could have spent 30 minutes or 10 minutes inside the UFO, correct?

Manuel: I don't remember. I have the feelings that I could have spent more time, where? I don't know? How much? I don't know.

Question: What did you learn from all this?

Manuel: I learned that we are not alone. I learned that we are powerless against the aliens. I learned that aliens are not as bad as many people have said. I learned that our governments are not telling us the truth about aliens.

Question: Manuel, let me ask you a final question. Why did the aliens pick you up from 6 billion people living on Earth?

If the aliens had such an important message to humanity, why didn't they grab or abduct the President of the United States, the Pope, the Secretary of Defense, the editor-in-chief of the New York Times or The Washington Post, or Jay Leno or David Letterman?

Those people can spread their message, more effectively, more convincingly, and for sure faster? Right?

Manuel: You are wrong, sorry senior, you are wrong! I saw very important people inside the UFO. I told you about Bishop..., Governor..., and... They were there, I saw them. Those people are very important. Why me? I don't know.

Did Manuel tell the truth?

Did the aliens indeed, abduct Manuel?

Did he from the UFO's window see what he claimed he saw?

Were inside the UFO, eminent people like a bishop, a governor, a TV celebrity, as Manuel have claimed to have recognized?

I am not sure. Nevertheless, Manuel has experienced something extraordinary.

Is it a physical alien abduction or simply phantasmagoric visions, produced by a vivid imagination?

Perhaps, some sort of hallucination?

But what IF, a small part of what he told us did happen? Then what? What would or could be the outcome/results of such encounter or experience? Nothing! For few, would believe it, and there is nothing they can do about it. And many will ridicule Manuel and discredit the whole story. Why didn't the aliens give Manuel and/or the other abductees, any souvenir from their spacecraft? This would be a terrific proof of their existence, and undisputable evidence of such an encounter!

What is my personal opinion about Manuel's account? Well, Manuel has described something inside the UFO, that ONLY top echelon in the military (United States Air Force), and military scientists who worked on UFO government projects are familiar with, and/or know about!!

For instance, Manuel has precisely and accurately described several things inside the UFO, to name a few:

The shape of the seats in the UFO:

He was absolutely correct when he said: "All the seats looked alike. They are not like an airplane seats. They were round. They were not positioned in rows, you know, like seats in an airplane, one after another. They were positioned inside a large circle."

Government's secret files contain almost identical description of the seats inside an UFO, and especially a "circumference of seats" placing the seats into an oval alignment.

The secret files did in fact, contain such words:

a-Circumference of seats;

b-Oval alignment.

How did he know about this?

The shape and description of the windows of the UFO:

Manuel was absolutely correct when he said: "Each window was joined to another window by a glass sheet. It appeared to me as if the windows were big dots inside a mirror or a fiberglass panel."

De facto, only and only governments' secret files/reports on UFOs, contain a parallel description of UFO's windows.
No where else, the words "glass sheet", and "big dots inside a fiberglass panel" were ever mentioned!
Only, in governments' secret files. How did he know about this?

Weather/Climate weapons system, invented by the military:
Once again, Manuel is absolutely correct when he said: "Some bases have weapons systems that can change the climate and weather of Earth, and this is very dangerous because the whole Earth will be destroyed if its climate changes." Well, how did he know about secret military weapons capable of altering Earth's weather? The truth is, YES, the United States and Russia have successfully developed such weapons! And many were put to the test, and have dramatically changed weather's conditions, and Earth's regional climate(s).
They were used for military purposes!! But certainly needed for the national security of the United States. How did he know about this? You might say, it is obvious, Manuel read about these weapons on the Internet. True. But what is astonishing to me is the fact, that Manuel mentioned these weapons, 2 years before any report on these weapons was made public.
Only, a few military scientists knew about this secret project at the time, Manuel talked about "Weather's Weapons"!

Did the Grays help Earth's governments in developing weather's weapons?
Military contractors would deny any Grays' cooperation. They ridiculed the idea that aliens took part in any joint operations, black projects, or research program(s) administered by the Grays. Scientists will tell you that the weather's weapons were developed by leading scientists in the United States, and possibly in Russia.
And quite rightfully, they have all kinds of reports, statistics, laboratories research, grants from the United States government, and charts to back up their statements. Nevertheless, there are few scientists known for their unorthodox and avant-garde thoughts who strongly disagree.

They claim that the United States government made a deal with the Grays. They are hundred per cent sure that the United States made all sorts of deals with the aliens starting in 1947. Ironically, they failed to substantiate their claims.

Digging deeper into the matter, I found out that some futuristic weapons systems were either part of alien technology reverse engineering program, and/or a joint black-project meticulously carried out by military scientists and the intraterrestrial Grays.

b- The extraordinary account of abductee, Ralph M. (As is, word-for-word, and unedited):

(Verbatim, word for word and unedited): "I was abducted twice by the Grays. The first time it happened in 1992, and the second time in 2001. I was taken to an underground secret base. At the base I saw lots of military men, nurses, doctors, and aliens. I do not remember all the details of my first abduction.

But I remember very well what did happen to me in 2001.

On the way to the base, the alien Gray kept on telling us that we had nothing to fear, and that everything is going to be fine if we cooperate with them. We were 10 people aboard a spacecraft.

How did I get inside the UFO, I don't know.

I do not recall anything prior to this. Suddenly I wake up and found myself with a bunch of people inside a flying saucer, or some sort of a secret craft. I can't tell you for sure. Some of the people who were abducted like me were talking about UFOs. I did not see a UFO, but from the interior design of this thing, I figured out that the spacecraft could be a UFO, not an ordinary airplane. The alien aboard the spacecraft was nice to us and spoke slowly and softly. Sometimes, I could barely hear him.

For some reasons I was not afraid. I was rather curious and taken by the gadgets of the craft. I don't know how long it took us to get to the base. During the trip I felt that time has stopped. A strange feeling, to say the least. A feeling that stayed with me for years.

I never understood how I felt. I have no explanation. But what I felt was real. I have no reason to lie to you. I asked the alien Gray why am I here? Who brought me here, and for what reason?

The Gray replied that nothing bad will happen to any of us. I think he meant all of us, all the people who were brought inside the spacecraft. He opened a small black box and told us to look inside the box.

I freaked out. What I saw is something out of this world. Two little babies, maybe one week old, with small heads and big eyes. You can take it from me, those babies were not humans. They looked like stuffed dolls.

One of the women shouted with tears in her eyes, this is my baby. I didn't know what she was talking about. I thought she went berserk, or lost her mind, or something like that. She wanted to grab the box, but the alien Gray stopped her right away, just by looking at her, and this was weird too. I don't know what he did. The woman froze like an ice cube. Seconds later, she stopped to cry and changed her mood. Just like that. No one dared to talk to the alien, except me.

I asked him what is the meaning of all this? What is the big idea? Who are these babies? Why did he put them in the black box?

And I kept asking him why I was brought to the spacecraft? I told him I want to get out and right now. He remained calm, cold like ice. He did not show any emotion.

He turned his head like a robot and suddenly said, these babies are yours and ours. They are our children. Your children. The future leaders and saviors of your world. We need your help. You were chosen because we know you very well. We met before, but you do not remember. Do not be afraid. Nothing bad happened to you before, and nothing bad is going to happen to you now.

One woman asked him, I am two month pregnant, please let me go home to my husband and children, please.

The alien Gray told the woman that her baby now belongs to a superior race of beings who are much better than human beings. He also told her that many of all the new born babies are going to grow up as the new leaders of the world. A world of peace and prosperity.

The alien Gray told us that the future of humanity is going to change, and all humans will live in a better and a safer world.

He also told us that the babies we saw in the box were created from our genes and their genes.

I did not understand what he meant by their genes. And I didn't ask him to explain. I was frightened and scared to death when I saw those babies wrapped with a plastic bag inside the black box."

Well, well, well! A black box, babies' heads inside a black box, children of a future to be created and decided upon by an alien race! Great stuff. A fantastic science fiction material. Right?

Do you think that Ralph M. has invented this story? And what about this macabre "Black Box"? Did he fantasize about it?

The Black Box:

Not really, because many abductees told me that indeed, their Grays abductors did show them a black box, and pointed at babies' heads inside the box. So what is this Black Box? Why did the aliens show the abductees, the heads of new born babies inside the box? Is there a message behind this horrifying display?

Let me briefly explain to you the whole story of the Black Box, and how the new future of humanity, and global change are closely related to the babies and the infamous black box.

For decades, many abductees talked about a frightening little black box, the aliens hold in their hands, during the abduction process. This box was later called by abductees the "Alien Black Box".

It is a little black box, the alien abductors, (in some unspecified instances) show to abductees, point to it, and return to their spacecraft. It seems bizarre, but unfortunately it did happen, according to very reliable contactees and abductees.

Many abductees, including experiencers wondered what was the meaning of all this? Why the extraterrestrials did not explain to them the reason for showing them this box?

Well, they did, but abductees did not get it.

Inside the Aliens' Black Box:

The little aliens' black box contains a live fetus of a hybrid entity (creature), which is part human and part alien Gray. The aliens show the Black Box to their abductees, and point them to a small entity which resembles human beings; sometime, they are babies, and some other time, adult (Males and females).

47

The aliens don't say a word. They just open the box and display its content. The intention of the aliens is clear: Look and see how we can duplicate you and create your replacement! What the abductees see is essentially a holographic photo of their children; children they will give birth to, when impregnated artificially in the aliens' test-tubes. Simply put, the Grays are developing a new human race; a race called Grays-Humans Hybrids, destined to rule our world, and change our way of life.

Interviewing Ralph M. (As is, word-for-word, and unedited).
Question: You said that the alien told you "everything is going to be fine if we cooperate with them." Did he explain to you how to cooperate with them?
Ralph: No. But he warned us...he said if we do not cooperate, the human race will be destroyed.
Question: Did he explain to you how the human race will be destroyed?
Ralph: Yes he did.
Question: What did he say?
Ralph: He said they have sophisticated weapons that will wipe us out. He said they have weapons that will put us to sleep and make us loose our memory. They will incapacitate us. They will rewind time or stop it completely. And we will die because we will not be able to move, to walk or to do anything. We will starve to death.
Question: Did he explain to you how the aliens will rewind time or stop it?
Ralph: No, he did not. He simply said that time will stop, and everything will stop with it.
Question: Did you understand what he meant by that?
Ralph: No sir, I did not.
Question: You said "during the trip I felt that time has stopped. A strange feeling, to say the least. A feeling that stayed with me for years." What do you mean by "I felt that time has stopped"?
Ralph: Something I felt inside me. I can't explain it to you. I didn't know what time it was, how long it took us to arrive to the base, something like that, you know. And when I returned home, I didn't know what time it was either.

Question: Didn't you look at your watch?
Ralph: No. You mean when I was inside the spacecraft?
Question: Yes, and before you were taken to the spacecraft, and after you returned home?
Ralph: When I returned home, I began to remember something, few things, but not everything.
And yes, I looked at my watch and could not understand where and how I spent one or two hours without remembering what did happen to me or how I spent all this time and not remembering where I have been or what I have done. I felt that time passed by so fast, and I could not account for the time I lost.
Question: What do you mean by "the time I lost"?
Ralph: A missing time.
Question: You said that the alien "turned his head like a robot." What do you mean like a robot?
Ralph: I mean he could not move his head as we usually do. He had to twist his body to turn his head.
He was stiff like a machine, like a robot.

Did Ralph tell us the truth? How did he know about the aliens' Black Box? Did he fabricate this story? Not really, because many abductees spoke about an alien black box. How about that alien sophisticated weapon system capable of halting time? Did Ralph fantasize about it? Not really.
Anunnaki Ulema Kanazawa told me about a mind-bending alien technology which is capable of slowing down time, or prolonging it indefinitely. He said, "Imagine people accustomed to working from 9 am to 5 pm, going to work in the morning to a day that seemingly never ends.
Or an ambulance with a patient that needs emergency treatment never seeming to reach the nearest hospital.
What should be a five or ten minute ambulance ride takes five weeks to travel the same distance in normal time."

Why a global change is necessary?
Is it a false statement or a mind control tactic?
The Grays told their abductees, a global change is necessary because it will stop all atrocities on Earth.

I am very concerned with the Grays' statement, because if indeed, they are worried about us, and want us to live in a peaceful world, why didn't they do anything about it? They are highly advanced, and they have all the tools, opportunities and means to change our world, and stop man's violence and atrocities? In fact, they do not need the cooperation of a few abductees to do so!

They can do it right away and on their own.

Besides, the Grays themselves told their abductees, that once the abductees are outside their bases and UFOs, they would not remember a thing, meaning that they will forget everything they saw and heard.

Consequently, the Grays' message will be forgotten for ever! An abductee told me that the aliens Grays don't think much of us, including their abductees. Joy L., an abductee, said, "The Grays think we are really stupid, incorrigible and hopeless." Roy S., an abductee from Mississippi said (Verbatim): "The Grays do not understand us at all.

They think we do not have personal identity. They told me that humans are easily influenced by people in power, and have been endoctrinated to serve the powerful and the rich. If we do not take care of our own problems and take the initiative to limit the power of our leaders, we will never live in peace. They will help us, if we help ourselves, first."

Pam Martin, an abductee reported to Dr. Jacobs, that the Grays showed her scenes of devastation to cities and wildlife, which made her aware of human responsibility for the problem.

Martin said: "I don't know why they're showing it to me. I can get this off the five o'clock news. I already know this.

He (The Gray alien) says that this, had to avoid this, or this could be avoided, or this has to be avoided, or something like that. I don't know, I just get the feeling like they think we're really stupid. Like there's something wrong with us. I get the feeling like, when he conveys that to me, that he's looking at all of us like a group. It's like they're not blaming us, but like, they're holding us responsible. I keep getting the feeling like we're supposed to fix this as a group. He doesn't seem to understand how it works around here."

c-Fernando Alvarez's account:
Fernando Alvarez from Lima told me, verbatim: "One of the Grays talked to me like Padre Diego. He said we are responsible for all the bad things happening to us. He said humans are the problem. He said they will help us if we listen to them. But when I asked him how they are going to help us, he did not tell me. I thought maybe he did not understand what I said in Spanish. So, I asked him again. And he replied, we have helped you many times in the past. We have removed bad people from their government posts and jobs. We have saved Earth when an asteroid was falling toward Earth. We sent the asteroid away and prevented a big collision from happening. This could have killed millions, and possibly destroyed Earth."

Interview with Fernando Alvarez (As is, word-for-word, and unedited):
Question: Did the Gray tell you who has been removed from office? Do you understand my question?
Fernando: Si, yes. He did not tell me, no sir.
But he said that they have a group of people watching us and watching our governments. Governments everywhere, all over the world.
He said that many presidents and generals will be replaced by good presidents and generals.
Question: What else did he tell you? Did he show you any picture or something like that?
Fernando: Yes. He showed me many revolutions and wars.
Question: How did he show you revolutions and wars?
Fernando: On a big screen, pelicula.
Question: You mean like a film? Cinema?
Fernando: Correct, like a film.
Question: Where did you see this film?
Fernando: In front of me. I saw pictures on a screen.
Question: Can you describe for me this screen:
Fernando: It was big, gigantic. The pictures were moving on a screen made from glass, soft like a mirror.
Question: Are you sure it was glass?

Fernando: No, I am not sure it was glass, but something like glass.
Note: Possibly, Fernando by describing the screen as "a screen made from glass, soft like a mirror", he was referring to Holographic projection (s).

Fernando Alvarez's account corroborates what abductee, Lucy Sanders told Dr. Jacobs, and vice versa. Sanders said: "Now they have a screen in front of me. They're telling me something about the future. What must be known for the future.
I see a bomb going off. I see a crack in the world. There's lava coming out. I'm looking at it from above the world, and a big crack in the world. The world is turned and a crack came in it. And black clouds everywhere and bad wind. And people on the ground dead. I see dead bodies everywhere. This cannot happen. This will not happen.
This shall not happen. This must not happen. Only you can do something about it. Only you can do something about it. You must stop it. It is coming. We are coming. You must stop it. You must stop the destruction. Your good is our good."-As reported in Dr. Jacobs' work. (Reproduced with the written permission from Dr. Jacobs.) This scenario about Earth's total destruction and atrocities committed by human beings figures prominently in all the rapports, abductees had with the Grays.

d-Statement of Rima T.:
Rima T., told me: "The Grays love us, but cannot help us unless we help ourselves. They are not blaming us for our actions, because they know we are weak. But they did tell me that they are going to help if we stop destroying Earth. I felt that they are sincere. So I asked them, what can we do?
And how they are going to help us.
They did not tell me how they are going to help us. But they did mention that they have the solution to our problems, and they are going to change everything in our societies. And when I asked them, when this is going to happen? They replied very soon. I wanted to know more and I asked them again, how soon is soon? And they answered before other alien races come to Earth.

I got very excited and I asked them about the other alien races they are talking about. And they said the Anunakui, *sic* (Anunnaki).
I did not understand what they meant. I asked them about those Anunakui *(sic)*, and they told me that the Anunakui *(sic)* are trouble makers, they are vicious and they are going to control us.

Interview with Rima (As is, word-for-word, and unedited):
Question: Why do you believe that the Grays love us? Did they show you any emotion or a genuine feeling toward you?
Rima: One of them hugged me. And I felt good.
Question: What else did he do?
Rima: He asked me to look outside the window and see for myself how miserable we are. He said, everything is going to change. There will be no more wars.
I really felt that he cares about us, how we live, and what is going to happen to Earth if we keep on destroying the environment.
Question: What window are you talking about?
Rima: The window of their UFO.
Question: You were inside a UFO?
Rima: Yes. It is beautiful. It is wonderful.
Question: Where you alone?
Rima: No. Many people, men, women, children were there too. And all looked very happy.

In comparing notes with Dr. David Jacobs findings, I found parallel statement given by Kathleen Morrison, an abductee who reported her abduction experience to Dr. Jacobs.
Dr. Jacobs wrote: "Kathleen Morrison's personal-project hybrid told her humans did not understand that their actions had effects beyond themselves. Although humans were a "hindrance" to the planet, he did not suggest corrective action.
During this exchange, Kathleen was looking at the stars from a UFO's window while her hybrid embraced her.
It is gorgeous up here. Reinforces how tiny we are, how tiny our concept is. In less than a blink of an eye, we are born and die. We have many opportunities to screw things up in that time though. I'm in the full throttles of an embrace and this is wonderful.

I love feeling his arms around me. This might sound funny but he almost talks like he has a love affair with the Earth. "-As reported in Dr. Jacobs' work. (Reproduced with the written permission from Dr. Jacobs.)

The Grays' concerns: Earth's environment and safety.
Many ufologists and researchers in the field believe that the Grays have a vicious agenda, and their alleged concerns about Earth's environment and its safety are not genuine.
This is not totally correct.
For sure, the Grays have their own agenda, but to assume that they are not worried about continuous underground atomic tests and nuclear detonations is absurd. On numerous occasions, the Grays did reveal their concerns to American and Russian military scientists, and decision makers.
This is an absolute truth.
Grays and our government's officials (From the United States Air Force and NASA) met multiple times. Although, each meeting focused on several issues, the question of atomic/nuclear arsenal, and underground detonations dominated the scene of discussions and communiques.
Earth's environment and safety do not categorically imply air pollution, decimation of forests, and clean water. Far from it. The Grays "do not give a damn about our forests and the purity of our environment; water, air and Earth's ecology," stated a European military scientist working on black projects and weather weapons systems in the US and England. He added, "They do not breathe our air...nor do they drink our water. They are afraid that what we are doing could blow up the whole damned Earth.
Do you blame them? They live here!!" In fact, the Grays have established their habitat on Earth, millions of years ago, long before man walked on the surface of the globe. And the military know that very well.
It is quite reasonable to conclude that the Grays are seriously concerned about Earth's safety, simply because they share it with us.
As reported by abductees, the Grays are fully convinced that we are violent, vicious, wars lovers, and annihilators of civilizations.

Therefore, "Earth's environment" should be understood as the safety of planet Earth, and continuity of life on the surface of Earth and beneath (Underground).

Did the military understand the Grays' message?
You bet! In 1992, the Grays met twice with civilian delegates, scientists and military men (Two Generals and one Lt. Colonel) from our government, in Arizona and Alaska. And they reached a final agreement. Should I say, a total/complete understanding that all underground nuclear testings should cease immediately? As a result, the United States stopped underground nuclear testings in 1992. Other leading countries followed suit.
England's last nuclear testing occurred in 1991, Russia in 1990.
France and China had a surprise-visit by the Grays in 1996. And before the end of 1996, both France and China abandoned their nuclear testings.
In 1998, Pakistan and India were confronted by angry Grays, when both country detonated their atomic bombs in the same year. The Pakistani and Indians got the message of the Grays.
Well, how about North Korea's nuclear test that occurred on May 25, 2009? We don't know.

Confusing abductees and sending them mixed messages:
Numerous abductees told me that the Grays gave them mixed messages before they were taken to a medical operating room. By mixed messages, they meant beautiful images of people and places, and horrifying scenes, concurrently.
For instance, one holographic projection showed scenes from a better future, where everything "seemed right and beautiful." And short after, the Grays projected horrifying scenes of wars and destruction from our future.
Why the Grays want to confuse their abductees, and send them mixed messages? It is not entirely clear. A serious researcher from Berlin, Germany, who is an anthropologist and military scientist, who previously worked on highly classified material, told me, verbatim: "The Grays purposely rewind time, past and future, to convince their abductees of their powers and intent to create a better world. The Grays have no sense of time.

55

However, they can clearly differentiate between past events and future events. The Grays don't follow any chronological order or time-frame sequences when they project holographic images.
Are they deliberately confusing their abductees?
I don't think so." A colleague of mine who previously worked at Institut Pasteur, in Paris, France said, word for word, "Quite often, abductees are confused by the variety and speed of images they see on a holographic screen. It is not always the message, but the intent of the Grays that confuses them."

My personal opinion: It is not in the best interest of the Grays to confuse the abductees. The Grays have no intent to confuse the abductees, simply because, the abductees were already confused by the whole experience. Anybody would be confused, if he/she has been subjected to such an extraordinary incident.
The confusion usually begins, as soon as the apparition of aliens occurs; long before the Grays lift up, levitate, and abduct people.

Most certainly, more confusions will follow up, when:
- a-The abductees enter a spaceship out of this world.
- b-The abductees are shown large holographic images and footages.
- c-The abductees are directed to an operating room.
- d-The aliens place them on a surgical bed.
- e-The abductees see strange aliens operating on them.
- f-The aliens show them the "Little Black Box".
- g-Etc.

All these sequences, events, and related phases of the abduction confuse the abductees. It is not exclusively the message or the speech of the aliens that confuse the abductees, but the whole process.
Can the abductees do something about it? Can they clear their minds and get rid of the confusion? Unfortunately not. They are at the mercy of the Grays. They are under the full control of the Grays, and there is nothing they can do to free their mind, understand what is going on, and to stop the abduction.

Many ufologists and so-called ufology-therapists have claimed that something can be done about abductees' confusion, and resisting the psycho-somatic effect the Grays have over their victims. Nonsense! The Grays have at their disposal all the mental, intellectual, scientific, paranormal, and physical means and tools to paralyze, handicap, incapacitate, and control the physical, mental, emotional, and psychological faculties of the abductees. Nothing can be done in this regard.

e-The account of Sal Luis Montez on the Grays' holographic projections of cities, they wanted him to see:
Sal Luis Montez said (Verbatim and unedited): "It was really beautiful. The streets were spotless. The houses had balconies with so many flowers beds. The sky was blue. And happy parents walked down the streets with healthy and well-dressed children. It was like a dream. I wished I could spend the rest of my life there."
Then, a few moments later, everything changed, when "the aliens projected frightening images from a far distant future... pictures of ruined cities, starving people, and so many soldiers mutilated by wars..." added Sal. "I did not understand the meaning of all this. Why did they start showing me beautiful things, and later on...nothing but wars, cities in rubbles and people dying from starvation?" continued Sal.

f-The account of Patricia Lorensen:
Patricia Lorensen, from Sweden, said verbatim, "First, I was shown gorgeous gardens with magnificent marble fountains, well-manicured loans, green green trees, happy peanuts vendors, strolling musicians, you name it, it looked like a paradise, and short after, everything vanished, no more gardens, no more fountains, no more nothing...and out of the blue, people in uniform appeared right in front me and ordered me to kneel. I did not know what to do.
I looked around me and saw a huge explosion, fume and dark smoke all the over the streets and shops' signs. It was like a war zone. I became so confused and totally disoriented. I didn't know what to do, or what to think.

I asked him (The alien Gray) what is going on, and he said, don't worry, now you saw everything; the good future and the bad future. It is up to you to decide where you want to live. We can help you if you give us good babies.

I became more confused because I was neither married nor pregnant. When I asked him how can I do that, and why should I do that, he said I was chosen, and they knew who I was.

He also said that it is going to be very easy, and would not take long. I did not know what he was talking about.

What did he mean by it would not take long? Without asking him any question, he explained to me what I have to do, and how it could be done so quick. I felt he was reading my mind. He came closer to me, and I think I fainted right away. Later on, I found myself lying down on a metallic bed in some sort of a clinic. And I fainted again, because I think they did something to me. I don't want to talk about it anymore..."

g-The strange and unusual account of Penelope Gambier:

Penelope-Bernadette Gambier, originally from St. Cloud, France, and currently living in the United States had a totally different experience. Reluctantly she admitted that she was abducted by aliens who looked like "strange little creatures with big eyes and without hair, a mouth or a nose", she said.

Interview with Penelope-Bernadette Gambier (Word-for-word and unedited):

Question: Where did you see these strange little creatures?

Penelope: In Gaithersburg, Maryland.

Question: What where you doing there?

Penelope: I go there to see my friends and ride horses.

Question: Where you alone when you saw these creatures?

Penelope: No, Gilbert and Sophia were with me.

We all saw the same thing, small creatures, two small ones and a miniature of a small child, very little.

Question: What did you do when you saw the small creatures?

Penelope: At first, we did not know what to think. The truth is, at the beginning, we were not afraid, it might seem strange to you, but you have to understand it was around Halloween, and we thought they were people in Halloween costumes.

But then, when they started to levitate, we began to wonder.

Sophia looked at me and said, something wrong here, she got scared and ran away. Gilbert could not move, but he could still see me, he froze like a stick.

Later on, he told me that he saw everything, he heard everything, but he could not move.

Question: Then what?

Penelope: Then, I became scared, what do you except?

When I saw Gilbert incapacitated, I freaked out.

I tried to run away, but I couldn't. Something grabbed me but I could not see it. I felt it but I could not see who was grabbing me.

I start to cry, I panicked, I begged them not to harm me.

It is a frightening situation, you will never understand how I felt unless you experience the same thing. You feel helpless, lost, confused, scared to death, nobody is there to help you, you are alone, you know what I mean.

I will never forget that night as long as I live. I told what I saw that night to a friend of mine at L'Alliance (Alliance Française in Washington, DC), and she thought I lost my mind.

Question: And what happened next?

Penelope: I start to float in the air like a feather. I did no feel my weight. I was less than a meter above the ground, maybe a little bit more, and suddenly a blue beam came at me, and began to lift me higher and higher, and I do not remember what happened to me next.

Question: How were they dressed these little creatures? First, let me ask you this, how big or how small were the creatures?

Penelope: The little creature, the very small one was of the size of a toddler, a little bit bigger than three year old baby. The others were four to five feet. I couldn't tell whether they were male or female. They looked identical. Three of them had a silver metallic suit. No zippers, no pockets, no belts, no buttons, nothing.

It appeared to me that their suits were part of their bodies. For a few seconds, I had the feeling that one of them was moving inside his suit and I though my God how bizarre this thing is!

Question: Did they talk to you?

Penelope: Not a single word.

Question: Did the blue beam take you somewhere?

Penelope: Yes. To a hospital.

Question: What kind of a hospital? Where?
Penelope: A military hospital.
Question: How did you know that?
Penelope: I saw people, men and women, doctors and nurses in military uniforms. Some nurses had white aprons, others white aprons or something like that with military insignia...I don't know what kind, but they were definitely of a military type.
Question: What kind of military uniforms?
Penelope: I don't know. Something very new to me.
I know how to recognize American military uniforms and I know French military uniforms too, but no, no...the medical staff and officers were not Americans...not French either. They looked just like us, but I saw at the corner of a room, a very short person wearing a plastic suit, white-beige in color, and another short guy wearing an ugly mask with two big holes in the front, and two tubes coming out from both sides of his head. These two creatures operated on me.
Question: What do mean they operated on you?
Penelope: Yes they did.
Question: Can you tell me more about the operation?
Penelope: The two little men approached me. Both were wearing surgical masks. One of them, removed the tubes that they were attached to his head and plugged them into an instrument, not far from my bed. Then, he turned a knob on a small panel. The other one asked me to relax. He spoke to me in French; mind you a very good French with an impeccable accent. In my whole life I have never seen a tiny person, and as short as a small chair, talking in French. I thought I was dreaming.
But then, when he placed a device over my head and started to tell me lots of things about myself, my parents and the things I liked most, and how he is going to relieve me from the lower back pain I had for years, then, and only then, I began to relax. He told me he is a doctor and he has helped many people like me.
Then, he asked me to look at a rectangular screen, not too big, not too small, and said to me, you are going to like what you are going to see. I interrupted him and asked him, why I was brought to this hospital. He replied that I need help.

60

I asked him, what kind of help? What's wrong with me? Who has authorized this? He replied, don't talk much, and just look at the screen. I continued to look at the screen, and photographs began to appear on the screen, followed by a footage from a war scenes. He asked me, do you recognize this?

I replied, no. He said, this is the French-Algerian war. You see how bad it is? The French army killed many innocent people in Algeria.

I asked him why is he showing me this? He said, the human race is violent, what they know and what they do best is war! Then, he said very calmly, pay attention to this...photos of Napoleon Bonaparte and La Grande Armée (The army of Napoleon as it was called back then) and troops appeared on the screen. I saw the Pyramids, the Sphinx, and Mameluk soldiers. He commented like this: "This is your emperor, he was bloodthirsty. Look, look at all these soldiers, they are wounded, covered with blood, dead, suffering....their ears cut off."

He stopped for a few seconds and said, but we have good news for new. We are going to change all this.

The other person came close to me, and attached a tube to my head and said, everything is going to be fine. He asked me to continue to look at the screen. Now the sceneries have changed. What I am seeing now is angels, women in labor, beautiful valleys, puppies, all mixed up together. And all of a sudden, photos of my parents, my friends and the home I wanted to buy in Bethesda appeared on the screen. I was absolutely fascinated by all this, but could not understand a thing. How this could be possible? How did he know about my parents, and the house I wanted to buy?

Then, I saw a baby smiling at me. He was different from all the babies I have seen in my life. He did not look completely human. In a way he was prettier than all the babies I have seen, but I have noticed something very unusual about his head.

The small creature told me, "This is your baby and our baby. He is going to become very important, and he will rule many lands. This is why you are here, and you are going to be part of our program. You were chosen. You have helped us in the past, and you are going to continue to do so.

We will take care of your son. You will come to visit him. We will educate him, and prepare him to become a good leader. You will spend a few days with us, and we will return you home safe. We will revisit you when necessary. And we are going to help you buy the house you like."

When I returned to the same place, from where originally I was abducted, Gilbert was still there. I found him in a state of trance.

He regained his senses, and asked me if something or anything strange had happened, he looked around and asked me again where is Sophia? I told him about what I went through. He nodded his head and said, "I believe you, do not say a word to anybody. No one should know, nobody should know about this."

Then, he said, "We must find Sophia, she disappeared. I hope she is not hurt." We looked everywhere and could not find her. Back then, we did not have cellular phones. We stopped the car near a convenient store and phoned her.

No answer. Then we called Alain, her boyfriend. He said that he does not know where Sophia was. The following day, I received a telephone call from Johns Hopkins University Hospital in Baltimore. The woman on the line told me that Sophia has been admitted to the hospital, that everything is fine, and I can come to see her between 10:00 AM and 4:00 PM. And that is my story. C'est tout!"

h-Interviewing Zarah Arslan (Verbatim, and unedited):
Question: Last time, you told me, "The aliens are spiritual beings who are coming to earth to save us." You also said, "They are going to change our world, and all the rotten rules and laws we follow, and create a new order." Do you remember that?
Zarah: Yes I do. When I said aliens, I meant the new race they are creating. They want to stay neutral. But the new race they created will bring the change I told you about.
Question: You mean, the hybrids who are genetically created by the aliens are the ones who are going to save the world?
Zarah: Yes, the hybrids, not the aliens.
Question: How did you know that?
Zarah: The aliens themselves told me that.
Question: What did they say exactly?

Zarah: They said, they have no intention for interfering in our affairs. They have all the powers to interfere, but they are not interested. My guardian assured me that they could have done it thousands of years ago, but they were waiting for the right moment. And the right moment as he explained it to me, is when a new race is created by them, a race which resembles us; a new race which will be integrated in our society.

Question: What do you mean by "my guardian"?

Zarah: The being of light.

Question: Being of light? Meaning what? A spirit, an angel, a super being?

Zarah: A spiritual alien. There is no such thing as angel and super being.

My guardian warned us against the propaganda of organized religions. He made it clear to us that we are all equal. He said that we are immortal and the seeds of the universe. But because we have lost our spirituality and became materialistic, we have lost our awareness and many of our powers.

Question: So, the hybrids are going to change our future. Did your guardian tell you, how they are going to achieve that?

Zarah: He said the hybrids know what to do, and we should not be concerned.

The hybrids are also beings of light, they are highly intelligent, and spiritually developed. They will become part of our daily life and guide us toward a cosmic awareness.

They will be everywhere, around us, in the government, in our schools, in our hospitals, everywhere. They are going to teach us many things, new things, and open our eyes on the truth which was distorted by religions and greedy leaders.

Question: Where did your guardian come from? And would it be correct to call him a Gray alien?

Zarah: Yes...

Question: Let's go back for a moment to what you have said before about why the aliens are not interested in interfering in our affairs.

Are you telling me that the aliens have never interfered in our business, government's affairs, genetic programs carried in secret bases, abductions, etc., etc.?

Zarah: They told us very precisely and clearly that they are not going to interrupt our lives. They are not coming to wage wars against us, and change everything right away. Our government is fully aware of their intentions and plans. They told us that many of the useful and good things, tools, and machines we use today in our industry, telecommunication, schools, hospitals, business, economy, transportation system, medicine, health fields were given to us by them. Many of the great inventions we see today were developed by them, and given to our governments and scientists, decades ago. They gave us lots of things. But they stopped a few years ago, because our government refused to serve the best interest of our society. They gave our government and scientists wonderful stuff...very advanced technology that could solve many environmental and energy problems, but our government refused to use them.

Question: Well, if the aliens care so much about us, why don't they interfere right away and save the world? They don't need the permission of governments. What are they waiting for?

Why don't they land right now and stop all wars, and put an end to all the atrocities we are suffering from?

Zarah: You don't understand...you don't. We have to wait for the right moment.

Question: What right moment?

Zarah: The right moment will come when the race, I mean the hybrids they are creating are ready to assume their duties.

They told us that we are not yet ready for this, ready to deal with the hybrids. A major change will happen, but first, the hybrids, I prefer to call them the beings of light, are not enough in number to oversee everything. They also told us, that physically and spiritually we are not ready. This is going to take a while, maybe years, I don't know. First, they have to prepare us mentally, spiritually and technologically. This makes perfect sense to me.

Question: Zarah, you are an intelligent woman, right? Educated and very successful. Do you really, honestly believe, the aliens or the beings of light as you call them, spent so much time with you and the abductees, just to announce their grandiose, loving, and humanitarian plan, and as you have told me before, they came back so many times to talk to you about the same thing?

64

Why would they convey their message to a bunch of people, instead of contacting CNN news desk, the BBC, or Public Television? This would be faster, more effective, and surely it would reach a wider audience. The whole world would know about their fabulous plan for humanity? Do you see what I mean? Or perhaps, you feel that you were chosen, and a few of us deserve such an honor?

Zarah: I just told you, humanity, people, the church, the media, the government, the whole world, people in the streets, even teachers and bright people are not ready yet to welcome them, to understand them, and accept a new way of life.

i-Interviewing Beatrice Perrin (Verbatim, and unedited):
Question: How many times have you been abducted?
Beatrice: Many times, since I was 5 year old.
Question: What did you learn from your abduction experience?
Beatrice: Many things. But before I answer your question, I want to explain to you something very important.

You might call it abduction, but in reality, I was not abducted all the time. Sometime, I was invited. I am not the only one who can say that. I have friends from Belgium and the United States who would tell you the same thing. If you have been abducted –the first time- when you were a child, expect to be revisited by the aliens in the future. The first experience was an abduction. But what followed wat not. The aliens would stay with you for the rest of your life. And you will receive messages from them quite often. I don't mean every day, but now and then.

They establish a strong bond with us. They create a relationship with those who are fit. Not all of the abductees are revisited by the aliens, because the aliens are looking for something very specific, like for instance, the type of blood, the genes, something like that.

I learned plenty from them.

For example, they told me that:
- 1-They lived here for millions of years. Way back, before the Ice age, during the Ice Age, and after the Ice Age.

- 2-They came from Zeta Reticuli and other planetary systems.
- 3-They keep contact with their people living on other planets.
- Some are in galaxies not yet known to us.
- 4-Our history is wrong. Many important events were left out.
- Historians did not record everything, because they were self-serving.
- 5-Humanity civilization began 65,000 years ago. But its history was lost, because our ancestors did not write it down.
- 6-Earth's civilization began with extraterrestrials who came to Earth from other planets. Mu, Atlantis and a few islands in the Aegean sea were the first colonies of the extraterrestrials, but ecological catastrophes wiped out their civilizations.
- 7-They had a big fight with the Anunnaki in Africa and in the Middle East. The Anunnaki used nuclear weapons to destroy their cities in Palestine, Turkey, and Africa.
- 8-Death is misunderstood by us. We never die.
- Our energy, which is part spiritual and part mental transforms itself after our body dies.
- 9-All religions on Earth are fake.
- 10-There is no heaven and no hell.
- 11-Reincarnation is a myth.
- 12-God did not create the universe.
- The universe created itself and did not start with the Big Bang.
- And there are many universes within multiple universes.
- 13-They have improved the quality and standards of our lives.
- 14-Many governments know about their existence, because they met many times, and gave our governments a highly advanced technology.

- 15-They had a fight with American soldiers in two secret military bases. Many American soldiers were killed.
- 16-The story of the crash of a UFO in Roswell is distorted. Their spaceship crashed not because it was hit by lightening, but because it missed the time-opening of a time-space pocket.
- 17-When the spaceship pilots decided to return home and exit the atmosphere of Earth, the scapeship hit a close door, they call it space-time tunnel. This is how and why the spaceship crashed.

Question: Are they still here?
Beatrice: Definitely. They never left, because they live here.
Question: Where do they live?
Beatrice: They have a huge network of cities, fully equiped with everything they need, houses, schools for their children, hangars for their spaceships, laboratories, houses for their families.
Everything, I mean everything.
They live underwater, inside the Earth, and on the surface as well. Those who live on the surface are humanoids, I know you call them hybrids. They don't like to be called hybrids.
They fully understand that they are not 100% humans, but soon, they will look like humans and act like humans.
Question: Are they in contact with our government?
Beatrice: What government are you talking about?
Question: The U.S. government?
Beatrice: Ah! I see. Not only the American government. They have contacts with Russia, Great Britain, and Mexico.
Question: Mexico?
Beatrice: Absolutely. They have a big base in Mexico.
Question: A base in Mexico? What for?
Beatrice: For scientific research. And the Americans are part of it.
Question: Do you have a map of their cities? Photos?
Beatrice: No I don't. But I have been there.
Question: There? Where?

Beatrice: In Mexico, the English Channel, Australia, Alaska, Arizona, Nevada, Malta, Russia.

Question: Why did you go there? What did you do there?

Beatrice: All sorts of things.

Question: Such as?

Beatrice: We receive orientation programs. They teach us about humanity's history and what is going to happen to us in the future. You know, they are monitoring us. They know everything about us. And they are working with the Americans and the Russians on a very important project, something to do with our future, space programs, the environment, and global change.

Question: A global Change? What do you mean?

Beatrice: I mean they are going to change the way we live, because it is self-destructive, and it is endangering our lives and their lives.

Question: Why don't they publish their project and send it to schools and universities, research centers, laboratories, the media, Hollywood? Everybody would benefit from it. Right?

Beatrice: They will. But we have to wait.

If they tell the world, right now, what is going on, and how things will change, many people will go crazy, it will confuse and scare millions, it will create mass hysteria, panic, and everything will stop, because people would not know what do do. But it is going to happen. They told us that they will reveal themselves to the whole world by 2020 or 2021.

Question: Did you have any intercourse with them?

Beatrice: Why are you asking me this question?

Question: Because many abductees claimed that the Grays had sexual relationships with their abductees. For some reasons, it was necessary to create a new human-hybrid race.

Are they lying?

Beatrice: No I did not. This is ridiculous. I don't want to answer this question.

Question: Why do you believe so much in them?

Beatrice: Because they have showed me things. Important things. Stuff I did not study in school. Or...let me ask you something. Do you think what you have studied in school about history, Jesus, Buddha, Moses, Egypt, is true?

Do you think the Church is telling us the truth? Do you believe in the Holy Spirit, heaven and hell? All this crap?
Do you believe everything you read in the Bible?
The Exodus story, for example? It never happened.
Nobody could find one single Israelite artifact in the Sinai.
Yet, the Jews or Hebrews if you prefer, spent 50 years, sorry 40 years in the desert. Not even one bone, one skull! Where did they bury their dead? No cemetery, no skulls, no bones, no nothing.
Don't you find this strange?
Our history is wrong! Our religions are fake!
Do you believe Jesus is the son of God? Well?
People don't believe that extraterrestrials exist because they don't show up themselves, because they don't land on the White House loan and talk to the President of the United States.
Did God land in front of the White House?
Did God reveal himself to us? Where and when?
How does he look like?
The aliens spoke to us. I know what I saw and this is more than enough for me to believe that they exist. I have an uncle who worked in Canada on a top secret military program, some 20 years ago, maybe more...He told me the Canadians and the Americans were building a fleet of UFOs. My uncle is an engineer of a first caliber and an honest man.
He told me that. When I asked him what did happen to these UFOs, he said, the Americans ceased their operations in Canada and moved all their files, cabinets, blueprints, spacecrafts, hangars, engineers and military personel to the United States, where they continued to manufacture those UFOs in a huge quantity.
He also told me, that in the United States, the aliens worked with Americans and English engineers, and showed them how to improve on these spaceships.
The aliens gave the Americans, extraterrestrial technology and know how.

A very special kind of relationship.
Grays helping abductees and saving the lives of hybrids:

The abductees spoke about a very special kind of relationship they had with the hybrids and the Grays. For instance Helene Rafi described how the "Grays cared so much for the babies hybrids placed for adoption, and who fell sick." She added, "two hybrids babies became seriously ill, and for some reasons, they were no longer able to breathe.

The military family who adopted them tried everything, and all their efforts remained in vain. Then, the Grays told the parents to take the babies to Walter Reed Hospital, Army Medical Center, in Maryland, where they would operate on them. The parents did without hesitation, and the Grays doctors operated on the babies and saved their lives.

Another example was given to me by abductee, Margee B., who said, "During the New York City Blackout of 1977, millions had no electricity in their homes, apparently caused by a lightning strike, except for two native American families who have adopted hybrids children. The whole neighborhood was dark, but you could see light only in these two houses. Nobody could figure it out. It is really mind boggling."

Abductee Emily S. said, that she saw women and children crying and crying, and were scared to death by the whole thing. The alien asked her to go and talk to them, and tell them that they have nothing to fear. Another alien gave her a box of candies and told her to give it to the children.

It appeared to her that the aliens were concerned, and did not want to see the abductees upset or afraid. Emily was assigned the duty of watching over the children, and make sure that all the abductees felt good. The aliens told her that she is now one of their assistants. According to Emily, the aliens' intent was to create a friendly community, where everone would feel safe and happy. In some instances, the aliens would give the children, toys and chocolate bars.

Emily said, that she did not feel threatened by the aliens. They treated her well, and never ordered her to do anything, except once, when she tried to remove the blue apron they gave her.

Aprons of different colors and sizes were given to the abductees for very specific reasons.

j-Interview with Emily S (Verbatim, and unedited):
I asked Emily why the aliens didn't use telepathy or other means to calm down the abductees. She replied, "Oh no, aliens don't use force or telepathy with children. They are very considerate."
Question: Do aliens eat chocolate?
Emily: They don't. They don't eat at all. I have never seen any of them eating anything.
Question: They don't eat at all?
Emily: This what everybody said.
Question: Do they drink?
Emily: I am not sure. I don't know.
Question: But they had chocolate bars.
Emily: It is for the children. They love children; our children and their children.
Question: Do the aliens (The Grays) impose a strict policy upon the abductees?
Emily: Only in the refectory, and children playground area. They want the parents to teach their children how to behave. The aliens want to create for all of us a family environment, healthy, clean and friendly.
Question: Why only in the refectory, and children playground area?
Emily: Because we eat all together.
And they don't want the children to get into a fight with their children, I mean the hybrids children.
Theirs are much much calmer and polite than ours. They want to keep the playground area spotless. They don't like messy stuff. The aliens are very hygienic.
Question: Who clean after the children, yours and theirs?
Emily: Everybody. Us, the adult hybrids, the mothers, but not the aliens.
Question: How do the aliens feed the babies?
Emily: They ask the mothers to breastfeed them.
Question: Mothers hybrids?
Emily: No, us, humans.
Question: And how the mothers feel about that? Breastfeeding aliens?

Emily: They become very attached to the babies. As I told you, it is like a family.

Question: So, there is no more distinction between human children and hybrids childen?

Emily: None whatsoever.

Question: Did you breastfeed any of those babies?

Emily: No.

Question: Why not?

Emily: I could not. But they did help. They attached some sort of a sucking machine to my nipples and extracted milk. I couldn't believe it. It worked.

Question: The aliens did that?

Emily: No the adult hybrids. And they do more than that. They are constantly busy.

Question: Like what? What do they do? Busy with what?

Emily: They teach the hybrids children how to communicate with each other, with us, with the aliens.
They show us how to extract sperm from men using machines and other devices. They take us on tours to show us what is going on around us, outside the compound, and sometime, we board their spaceships and go visit places, all kinds of things.

Question: In what language do you communicate with the adult hybrids?

Emily: I talk to them in English and Spanish.

Question: And the others?

Emily: Same thing. I don't know. In any language.

Question: How do you communicate with the aliens?

Emily: Same thing.

Question: Do they speak English and Spanish?

Emily: Better than you and me.

Question: What do you talk about when you speak to the aliens?

Emily: Many things. Whatever I want.

Question: And they answer all your questions?

Emily: No, not really. Not all the time.
Sometime, they direct me to a screen inside a panel attached to the wall...on the screen, they print their answers and display photos, like a newsreel.

They are way ahead of us. They read your mind in a blink of an eye, and answer your questions either verbally or on the screen. And they want to make sure that you understood their message.
The aliens are not emotional like some hybrids, and the children of the hybrids. But they are not distant.
I mean they communicate with us, they tell us what to do, if we make a mistake, they instruct us how to correct our mistakes. They want us to feel good, but also to be efficient. They count on us to create a family atmosphere for their children. Although the adult hynbrids can do the job perfectly, the aliens believe a human touch is necessary.
I do understand their reasons, because soon or later, the hybrids children will become part of human societies, and many will be put for adoption.

k-Account of abductee, Claire Tibodeaux:
Abductee, Claire Tibodeaux, told me that both the aliens and the adult hybrids spend considerable time teaching the abductees.
Like a speaker, who in seminars, uses slides and charts, the aliens do the same thing. But they go one or two steps further.
For example, they train the abductees how to use their minds to change pictures projected on a screen, and they want us to succeed. Or, they ask the abductees to visualize in their minds, scenes or situations that could endanger the lives of hybrids children. And how fascinating it is to find out that the aliens already read our minds, and knew what we were thinking about. They do that by using a band attached to their forehead.
This band can read our thoughts. Why would they do that, if they didn't care? This is one of the ways they use to communicate with us, and try to establish a direct and sincere rapport with us. It is really very special.

l-Account of abductee Sloan (Verbatim, and unedited):
Scenes from the future:
"Aliens and mature hybrids alike, engage us in stimulating mental exercises. For instance, they show us on a huge screen, scenes from the future. And they tell us what is going to happen in the future. We better be prepared to deal with future problems and risky situations..." said, abductee Sloan.

73

She added, "On a huge screen, they show us, for example, a car accident, passengers were hurt, cars smashed, blood, shattered glass, smoke...and they ask us what are we going to do to help the injured people, or how to save lives.

Sometime, we see hybrids children trapped inside the cars, or bleeding to death. I think they are doing this on purpose to see how we are going to react, and save the hybrids.

They expect from us utmost loyalty to their children.

And they keep on repeating over and over, that the scenes are real, and will happen in the future.

They told us that our attachment to hybrids children should not be diminished, that our relationship to the community (Hybrids' community) is here to stay for ever.

A very special kind of relationship that will prove to be very useful when we return home.

A bond with the hybrids children should not be broken."

m-Account of abductee Rosalind M.:

The bond with aliens.

Abductee, Rosalind M., asked the aliens, about this bond, and how could be maintained when the abductees return home.

Will the abductees stay in touch with each other?

Will the hybrids or the aliens stay in touch with the abductees?

Will the abductees be able to see the hybrids children when they leave the community (Hybrids' community in their habitat), talk to them, or visit with them?

Will the abductees be informed about the new locations of the hybrids children?

Who adopted them?

Names and addresses of the families who adopted them?

The aliens did not give specific answers, however, they did tell Rosalind three important things:

1-The aliens will stay in touch with the abductees and the adopted hybrids children for ever. The role, the abductees should play in the future to insure the safety of the hybrids children will be carried on for a very long time. And periodically, the aliens will recontact the abductees, monitor their task (s), and provide additional guidance.

2-The abductees shall not be informed about the whereabouts of the hybrids childen, only their mothers and the adult hybrids who trained the children will remain in touch with them. But this will come to an end, when the adopted hybrids childen reach the age of maturity.

3-The hybrids childen who were integrated in human societies are expected/predestined to play important roles in their new environment, on so many levels, and thus, help humanity to reach a higher level of responsibility, knowledge, intelligence, and cosmic awareness.

n-Account of Patricia Selby-Hutton (Verbatim, and unedited):

- I asked him if I should believe in God? He said, each universe has its own god. Ours was created by ignorant and scared people. And religions used this created god to control their followers.
- I asked him if I should believe in the Final Judgement? And he said, each one of us will be self-judged.
- I asked him about reincarnation. And he said, you don't return to the same place if you haven't learned the truth in that place. You go somewhere else, where you can learn the truth and evolve mentally and intellectually. He said reincarnation is a nice story.
- I asked him if I should believe in horoscope and something like that. And he said, horoscope is a nice game, but could become a dangerous game, if we take it too seriously.
- I asked him if I should believe in hell. He said that we live in hell. I assume he meant Earth.
- I asked him if Earth will be destroyed one of those days. And he said, our universe will come to an end, soon or later.
- I asked him if finally, we will make contact with extraterrestrials, in the near future. And he said, we have already done that.
- I asked him if he was married. And he said he has children.

- I asked him if he eats food like us, and what kind. He said, he does not.
- I asked him if the hybrids were well-treated. And he said yes.
- I asked him who created us. And he said a race which made lots of mistakes, and created so much wars.
- I asked him to explain to me what he meant by a race which made lots of mistakes, and who is that race. He said the Anunnaki. They created us deformed and undeveloped mentally and physically. He considered this to be a serious mistake.
- I asked him if it is possible to correct their mistake. And he said, this is why they are here. He meant they came to us to help us.
- I asked him if he knew the Anunnaki. And he said. Yes, and it was not pleasant.
- I asked him why, and he said they are violent and destructive.
- I asked him if it is possible to visit with him. He said, I would die if I go there.
- I asked him why, and he said, atmospheric conditions. I would not be able to breath, I will suffocate. I will die instantly.
- I asked him how come the hybrids can live there. And he said, they are not humans.
- I asked him if he could read my mind, and he said yes.
- I asked him if he coul read the future, and he said yes.
- I asked him if he could tell me something about my future. And he said, it is not always wise to know the future.
- I asked him, how old was he, and he said 75,000 year old.
- I asked him if he believes in our Lord Jesus. And he said, Jesus was a good man.
- I asked him if Jesus was God or the son of God. And he said, no.

- I asked him if he believes in God. And said, Each civilization has its own god.
- I asked him to define God for me. And he said that I will never understand.
- I asked him why. And he said, because our mind is not developed enough to understand what God is.
- I asked him if he believes in the Virgin Mary. And he said, she suffered enough.
- I asked him if the Popes will go directly to heaven after they die. And he said, eventually all of us will end up in a better place.

0- Account of Richard P.:
Note: Synopsis of what he told me, word for word, as is, but with minor editing.
Note: "They" means aliens, Grays, and extraterrestrials.

What the aliens told Richard P.:
- The Earth was not always round. At the beginning, the Earth was shapped like an egg.
- There are 14 planets in our Solar System. Because of cosmic dust, space debris from the formation (Creation) of our universe, and strong atmospheric lights/flairs, we can't see them all.
- Earth is one of the dumpsters of the universe. And there are many.
- It is not the gravity that attracts planets and stars, and conditions their orbits, but the emptiness of the space, we call it dark matter.
- White Holes are stronger and larger than the Black Holes.
- Black Holes create universes and new worlds as we speak.
- There are old civilizations on the Moon and Mars.
- There are man-made military intallations on the Moon.
- They don't mutilate animals.

- The Germans built the first UFOS. Few flew at the very end of World War Two.
- The Americans have UFOs.
- The early pyramids are 10,300 years old. The first three (The biggest ones) were not built by the Egyptians. An early human race considered to be remnants of extraterrestrials, built the Pyramids with help from outer of space cvilizations. They mentioned the Anunnaki and the Lyrans.
- They have two underwater bases in Alaska.
- They have a base in Mexico, used by the Americans as a research center.
- They taught the American military how to use "Weather Weapons".
- The Philadelphia Experiment did happen. Thirty five seamen were killed.
- Atlantis, called back then Attara, did not sink to the bottom of the ocean. It desintegrated. It will never be found again. However, few rocks fragments are still visible.
- They can rewind time, but they can't re-start it.

p- Account of Merle O.:
Note: Synopsis of what he told me, word for word, as is, and unedited.
Note: "They" means aliens, Grays, and extraterrestrials.
What the aliens told Merle about holographic projections and holographic transportations:
The Americans conducted experiments and tests on holographic transportation.
Merle did not undertstand what the aliens meant by holographic transportation. He asked them if a holographic transportation is the hollographic projection he heard about. And the aliens said, these experiments are far more advanced, because not only a photo is projected hollographically, but the projection is:
- a-Animated;
- b-Live, meaning visual and audiovisual in a human form.

- c-The picture of the human form does in fact represent a human being.

In other words, a human being is transporated holographically, and can act, react, and respond like a real human being. Simply put, the holographic picture is a real human being in the flesh.

Merle asked: Is the holographic transportation physical?
Aliens' answer. Yes.
Merle asked: Can we touch a holographic person? Is it real, alive?
Aliens' answer: Yes.
Merle asked: Is the holographic person from our world?
Aliens' answer: Yes. It is. It was.
Merle asked: Is it from our future?
Aliens' answer: No. It is from your past and the present?
Merle asked: Is it a copy of a person from our present?
Aliens' answer: It is not a copy. It is a real person.Merle asked: Then, the holographic person from the past got to be a copy, because it is from the past?
Aliens' answer: It is a copy of a person from the past.
Merle asked: How could possibly a dead person return to life?
Aliens'answers: Dead in your dimension, alive in another.
Merle asked: Does a holographic person feel like a human?
Aliens' answers: Yes.
Merle asked: Can we talk to a holographic person like a real person, and ask questions?
Aliens' answers: Yes.
Merle asked: Would we get correct answers?
Aliens' answers: If you ask the correct questions.
Merle asked: Is it a projection on a screen or on a grid?
Aliens' answers: Inside a conic container.
Merle asked: How big is this conic container?
Aliens' answers: Big enough to accomondate a life-size human.
Merle asked: Can I go inside the container?
Aliens' answers: You will die.
Merle asked: Why? From what?
Aliens' answers: Radiations.
Merle asked: If the person inside the container is real as you said, can this person get out of the container?
Aliens' answers: Partially. Only the hands.

For a few seconds.
Merle asked: The person inside the container, is he created by a holographic process?
Aliens' answer: The person inside the container is a real person. The holographic channel allows the person to enter and exit the container. The channel does not create persons.
It transports them.
Merle asked: Can you create a real person?
Aliens' answers: You are not asking the correst question?
Merle asked: Can you create an imaginary person?
Aliens' answers: You are not asking the correct question.
Merle asked: Can you transport a ship, a car, a city, anything, besides a holographic person to a container?
Aliens' answer: Yes, we can.
Merle asked: How?
Aliens' answers: By creating a grid and transposing on the grid, the object we want to transport.
Merle asked: Can you move the whole City of New Orleans to Vancouver Canada?
Aliens' answer: We can.
Merle Asked: Did you tell the military how to do that?
Aliens' answer: We have already answered your question.
Merle asked: I did not get it.
Aliens' answer: Because you do not ask the correct question.

q- Account of Rick O.
The Grays told Rick:
- During the visitation (Abduction), few, who displayed exceptional intellectual and mental abilities will receive special training aimed at developing psychic powers, such as reading others thoughts, eliminating bad vibes emanated by others, and shifting the weather.
- All humans have positive energy and negative energy. The negative or "sick" bio-organic frequencies of the human body can cause electrical malfunctions, computers' crashes, and illnesses.

80

- The Grays help the abductees to get rid of their negative vibes.
- Humans' environment is not healthy.
- Humans lack harmony and synchronization in their lives. Asking the Grays if Feng Shui is helpful. And they said yes. However it is limited.
- The universe was created from within, it created itself. And the creation process is perpetual through the burst of multiverses. However, the universe, the humans know will come to an end.
- Spirits do exist. They have powers over matter and mind. They exist everywhere, on Earth, in holograms, in diagrams, and even in electricity.
  However, they have their own zone in other worlds. Some are aerial entities, others bio-organic.
- Orbs are not the manifestation of a soul, but the imprint of energy. All forms and substances of energies have orbs. Even plants, rocks, and water can produce orbs in multiple forms.
- Asking the Grays, if orbs are UFOs, and they said NO!
- Materialization of objects and presences is one way, highly developed entities use to announce their presence. Humans can materialize and dematerialize, because their essence is not physical. However, their greed and violence have become a barrier.
- They taught the Americans how to alter atmospheric conditions to improve the quality of the climate, but the military wanted to use it as weather weapons.
- The United States aim is to have complete military control over the earth.
- The military changed the weather improvement modules system they received from the aliens into laser weaponry, and it has become a climate-change arsenal.
- The Grays said that the multi-dimensional world they experienced is time-space continuum, where time is not linear.

- Anunnaki Ulema Ben Zvi said, there are time-space portals that lead to other dimensions, similar to geo-space-pockets on the perimeter of parallel dimensions that allow solid objects to enter and exit adjacent zones in the multiverse.
- Only through transmission of mind, and etheric exercises, mankind could perceive and comprehend these phenomena. In this context, it appears that koan meditation and mental enlightenment are needed to understand entities fluctuations, and extraterrestrial manifestations.

Changes in abductees' personality, and new beliefs:
Numerous abductees told me that their abduction experience developed in them, psychic powers, and the ability of reading others' minds. Jean-Luc Bernard said, verbatim, and unedited:
"I was abducted twice. After my second abduction, I felt that something has changed in me. Now, I can read others' thoughts, and guess right away what they are going to talk to me about.
I start to see numbers and images inside my head. I had a poor memory, but now, I can remember almost everything. My whole personality has changed. The aliens are not here to get us, as many people think. I had a wonderful experience."

"They helped me with my children."
Natasha S., said, word for word, "I was abducted many times. Nobody believed me. My friends thought I am going crazy. I am not. My two children were abducted too. And I thank the aliens for that, because now they are better at school. They helped me with my children. Igor was null in math, now he gets A in math and calculus. The aliens transformed him totally. He is brilliant now. He is now more clever than all the boys at school."

"They created a new baby for me."
Irma said, word for word, "I was 3 month pregnant and I lost my baby. The aliens told me I am going to be pregnant again.

But this time, they will save my baby, because they have changed my fetus. They showed me the picture of a beautiful baby and told me he is mine. When I asked them, who's baby is, because I did not intend on having a second baby, they said to me, they have removed my fetus, and replaced it with another one. I became very curious and I looked again at the picture, but could not find any resemblance.

They said, they have created a new baby for me and soon I will be pregnant again. Three months later, I became pregnant again without sleeping with my boyfriend. I asked my gynecologist how come I am pregnant again, since I did not have sex with anybody. The doctor assured me that yes, I was pregnant. I could not believe it. Six months later, the doctor delivered my baby, and he looked very beautiful, exactly like the photo the aliens showed me. This miracle has changed my life, and everything I believed in.

The aliens cured him from a lung cancer:
Ernest has been abducted numerous times. And he does not fear the aliens. In fact, he is grateful to them, because they have cured him from a lung cancer.

He has all the medical records to substantiate his claim. Ernest said, verbatim, "I am totally cured. It is a miracle. A big miracle. The aliens saved my life. If you don't believe me ask my doctor."

A brief interview with Ernest:

Question: So, the aliens are not so bad after all. Are they always good to people?

Ernest: They were good with me.

Question: Everybody is cured, like you?

Ernest: I don't know. But one thing I know...I know many people who were really stupid. But after they have been abducted, they became very intelligent.

Question: Can you explain this to me?

Ernest: The aliens work with all kinds of people.

Some are intelligent and educated, some are not. They put the stupid people on a program.

Question: What kind of a program?

Ernest: The aliens change the personality of a person, because they want us to become more important in the society. The aliens told us one day we are going to play important role in the society. They explained to us, to me, to everybody that what happened to us is not abduction...we were lucky because we were chosen. If we help them, they will help us.

Question: Did you ask the aliens how could you help them?

Ernest: Of course I asked them, and they said, the time will come when I will understand how I can help them, but for now, I must not be afraid of them. They told me not to have sex with my wife for six months. When I asked them why, they said because my wife was chosen and she must stay pure.

Stories, Reports, and E-mails, I received (As is, word for word, and unedited):

From Mr. Sam Bryar.

E-mail received on October 13, 2010. Time: 1:52 PM. Eastern Daylight Time. E-mail address: warrior007@speakeasy.net

"Dear Mr. de Lafayette,

Here is part of my story... Five and a half years ago, my mind was electronically attacked by way of microwaves, elf waves, and electroencephalography.

I became a target of harassment, gaslighting, gangstalking, etc. It was more laughable than scary. No one knew what they were doing, fortunately for me.

The attack involved transmitting their voices into my head by way of microwave hearing or voice-to-skull technology, which enables one to bypass the ears and talk directly into the auditory neuro-receptors of the brain.

I was also being given the shared dream experience, somewhat like in the movie, "Inception."

Well this attack opened a dimensional doorway into my brain and I started to communicate with people that weren't human.

Suddenly my shared dream experiences were more of extraterrestrial and underground kingdom origin. They made me part of their collective. They told me that I was indigo and that they needed to do things with me. Now regarding the less benevolent ET aspect to this, the Gray involvement.

It turns out that the Grays, Draconian, and Reptilians are running this operation by way of their disembodied and embodied white supremacists, mafia, and gangster minions. There are also CIA and NSA aspects to this as well.

I don't know if abduction was part of my experience or not, since it could easily be "memory-wiped", but the Grays tell me that I am not a part of that because as they say and I quote, "We don't do anything to people like you, because you know what you are."

That translates to myself being a higher awareness.

They use lower awareness beings for manipulation and behavior modification among other things.

They have used my libidinal energy though.

Now my experience has been vast. I've seen Grays walking through my home, mostly in apparition form.

While some of these beings can give you chills, other times the experience has been quite amusing, since I hear their voices all of the time. They have been in the United States since at least the 1930's or 40's and they are well adapted to

American culture, so to hear them swear like sailors or make a reference to something in pop culture, like a tv show or movie is quite funny. It's none of this, "Take me to your leader." or anything else that are given stereotypes.

They sound like everyday people.

My brain has connected to all sorts of types of extraterrestrials, extradimensionals, people of the underground kingdoms, and unfortunately some humans for five years and the experience has been exceptional. Now I also have much contact with hybrids. The hybrids have more human qualities and they don't really care for the full on Grays. Some of them live in the underground kingdom, where they escaped to or just left.

Some live at Area 51.

Those ones at Area 51 said that if I had a way to be there, my attackers "would get their asses kicked."

There are so many different things going on that I wonder if you would have any specific question that you would like me to answer. I have beings connected to me 24 hours a day. Maybe I could get a hybrid to answer any questions as well.

My truth is stranger that most people's fictions. In the meantime, all the best to you! -Sam Bryar

Interview with Sam Bryar (As is, word for word, and unedited):

Question: What did you mean by "I was also being given the shared dream experience"?

Sam: When I was first electronically attacked I was experiencing both visitations and manipulations in my dreams. I was put in certain types of scenes and situations.

Initially these dreams were simulated nightmares and human harassment. Later on they became visitations from women and then ultimately extraterrestrial extradimensional experiences.

I haven't had a single dream or private thought to myself since May 2005.

Humans have the technology electronically to manipulate and share in dream experiences. However many different beings exist on astral and extradimensional levels and when this door into my mind was opened these beings began to pursue me in large numbers.

Question: Could you please explain this to me "I started to communicate with people that weren't human"?

Sam: As this electronic harassment experience got started, the only people talking into my brain were humans. But soon later people were speaking to me in English, but their terminology was entirely different.

Certain communications were not conventionally making much sense. I knew that I had been no longer speaking to anyone human. They used terminology such as "house" for the word "body", which is the housing unit of the soul, rather than identify the body with who you are.

Question: What did you mean by "Suddenly my shared dream experiences were more of extraterrestrial and underground kingdom origin"? What underground kingdom are you referring to?

Sam: I was initially experiencing dream manipulation from human factions electronically.

Not long after that I started dreaming with communication in very fast disjointed English who would repetitively show me something a streaking fireball or meteor going across a vivid blue sky and then they would try to talk to me about it.

Some other times I would find myself somewhere like Telos, Shamballa, or Agharta with someone attempting to tell me something.

Question: You wrote, "They told me that I was indigo and that they needed to do things with me." What things? And who are they?

Sam: They are a collective of beings from both underground, other planets, and other dimensions. They are of a benevolent nature. They told me that I was an advanced spiritual incarnate soul and that such evolution could make my own personal merkaba beneficial to many beings as we approach the end of an upcoming cycle of transformation for this third dimensional earth. Some of them come to learn how to raise their vibrational frequency for such a transformation.

Others...more advanced ones want to show me the right way to things so that I may be of such assistance.

Question: Can you elaborate on your statement, "It turns out that the Grays, Draconian, and Reptilians are running this operation by way of their disembodied and embodied white supremacists, mafia, and gangster minions.

There are also CIA and NSA aspects to this as well."

Question: How do you know this?

Sam: Personal experience and lots of literature. They will even verify such things to me through my mind link.

They don't care. You may reference such things with Val Valerian's Matrix Series, Volumes 1 through 4, my electronic harassment website, www.emhdf.com, including a book by Fritz Springmeier and Cisco Wheeler at www.emhdf.com/Monarch-mind-control.pdf, Commander X's books -"The Controllers", "Mindstalkers", and "The Cosmic Patriot Files"

Question: Explain what do you mean by "The Grays tell me that I am not a part of that because as they say and I quote, "We don't do anything to people like you, because you know what you are."

Where did you encounter the Grays? What did they mean by "you know what you are"?

Sam: I encounter them every day. Mostly all contact with Grays are auditory in my experience, with visual contact from time to time. The Grays came with the white supremacist, mafia, gangster, and CIA aggressors, so when I became linked, they became linked. Now I have to hear Grays just about every day. As far as what, "You know what you are." means. Everyone non-human that I have encountered uses this terminology. They think on levels of awareness.

"You don't know what you are." means that you are an infant, a child, or an underdeveloped adult. There is a universal law that states that "awareness-of-an-awareness units"' free will must be respected and allowed to evolve. However, Reptilians and Grays found a loop-hole in that clause where they can persuade an "awareness-of-an-awareness unit" to consent to giving up their soul-mind-body complex for harvesting. The Grays want lower awareness for mind control, body manipulation, behavior modification, etc.

Question: You wrote, "They have used my libidinal energy though." How did they use your libidinal energy? Can you give me an example or two?

Sam: I really don't have an example for you. I don't know the process involved. The Grays are sensation deprived and if you have strong libidinal energy like I do they will feed off of it.

The human loses all sexual interest, stimulation and sensations. The grays will often flock to places of pornographic film making and prostitution, I have learned.

Question: You wrote, "While some of these beings can give you chills, other times the experience has been quite amusing, since I hear their voices all of the time."

Question: What do you hear exactly? Do you receive messages from them? What did they tell you?

Sam: Since I hear them everyday I hear a vast array of things. Maybe at some point you may ask me something and I will them.

Question: You wrote, "Now I also have much contact with hybrids." What kind of contact?

Physical? Mental? Telepathic?

And what did you get out of this contact?

Sam: Mental, telepathic, and from the shared dream state. I get that they want more contact with humanity. That they want to embrace their human side more than their gray side. They want some sort of love-based union with the human race.

People talking about their experience and encounters:
Note: Stories and Reports I received via E-mails.
As is, word for word, and unedited.
From Chris Smiley, Rescue Diver/USCG Lic. Captain.
Captain Smiley authorized us in writing to publish the following on October 12, 2010, at 7:53 pm.

George and I's close encounter.
I have seen some kind of hovering craft about 200 yards long hovering, w no wind or sound with a lull in the rain, we went out to watch the creek washing out the road we had just built and saw it when the lightning struck behind it several times.
An amber smaller rover looking craft or car or something crossed and circled the field and appeared to be traveling very smoothly across this mud pit of about 400-500 acre wheat field freshly plowed! It had to have been summer because this would have been the only time we worked down there.
There was phosphorous on the fence where we had seen the smaller object on the ground and had crossed the fence. Then we laid our .22 rifles down at the fence leaning them up against a cedar post by the two rungs of wire that were glowing with a green phosphorous glow very slightly in two pretty small spots and started in the direction of the object.
Well, we didn't get very far maybe two or three steps and we looked at each other without saying a word and backed out!
We weren't scared at all, but we weren't gonna get stuck out there in that mud either and especially without our rifles! We didn't want to get ourselves shot and we didn't know what this thing was so we couldn't shoot at it and we wouldn't have unless it jumped something or us.
The smaller object was separate from the very large hovering craft a few minutes before we approached the fence in fact it was what we saw first.

89

We couldn't imagine the neighbor's truck could be out in that field. This was back in the summer of 1978-'80 or so, with a friend I grew up with and still keep in touch with during and at the dead calm of an 11-inch in one-hour rainstorm front passing through one night in Hamilton, TX.

The lightning was thick and from cloud to cloud with long spidery rips and once in a while from ground to ground off o the East where it was heading off to, but the rain part had just passed us maybe five clicks to the East and the rain had stopped and there was, like, no wind, but the clouds above looked like they were churning and low like 500-1000 feet low and oppressive and dark, thick and black looking.

When we jumped the fence and began walking across the deep black double chiseled and double tandomed plowed field we sank to our knees in a few steps and both decided to move back and approach from the perimeter along the Southern creek side even though the water was raging and we decided this might be a real quick exit strategy too if this got any weirder.

The rover thing was about 450 yards away on the far side and just blinked out and then lightning stuck again behind the object. We saw it was huge and about mid field and sloped to the tree line like it was masking its silhouette parked tangent to the edge of the creek that headed due East and the hovering silent object with no wind or sound ran 300 yard sloping downward to the North and looked black and utterly non-reflective like flat "Black-hawk Black" but it didn't really look like a helicopter at all.

It looked like a disc with a height of about 50 ft. at the center and tapered about the same on both ends. It looked like it absorbed the light in contrast to the tree silhouette in the lightning compared to the bright flashed exposed behind it and there was no transparent views between the outside edges inside of the silhouette of the hovering object! It then had what looked like a line of low glowing red and Blue lights running along the leading 300 yard edge and was tilted slightly to blend with the terain in behind it as we aproached.

The two edged led looking line of lights looked like separate arms or something going down and up hinged at the outer edges and split down the middle.
He and I got within say 45-50 yards and were staying down in the gully in an ox-bow of the upper creek bed above the rushing water with a hump between us and the sound of the water, but no wind above the edge or any more rain.

The air was so thick you could cut it and the clouds seemed like the muffled all the sound around us, the lightning spiders were still going on but the ground lightning was fading to the East pretty fat and getting further and further between intervals and the sound of the thunder was fading it was probably 15-20 miles off by now, the rain.
We could hear nothing and feel nothing coming from the direction of the large object and as we peered over the edge into the field we saw its edges flex in two separate sections outlined by the low glow of the lights at the edges and the next time the lightning flashed within seconds it was gone, the both of them.
We waited for a little bit, but we didn't want to get caught again if it started raining again so we took off for our rifles at the fence and the house about 1/4 mile from the vantage point.

When we got back it was about 3 hours later than we both remembered it should have been, but we were just kids.
We didn't tell anyone about it when we got back to the house maybe a 1/5 a mile away and didn't talk to anyone else in the house about it to this day, but briefly some years later me and my friend brushed about it very briefly. We joked that maybe they picked us up and that was what was wrong with us "Dar He He" but all in all it was just some kind of joke.
We never spoke about it again. Well, I'm a hell of a tracker and so we went back to the cabin and went to bed. The clouds were black dark and ominous, but it didn't rain any more that night. The next day we went looking for a trail and anything on the ground would have left a major one.
All we found was our tracks in the grass, on the barbwire and where we set our rifles down and in and backing out.

91

It hadn't rained at all after we left and from the look of those clouds it sure should have even after raining 11 inches in the one hour! That was it.

Zip! Nada! No trail, tracks or anything and my eyes weren't lying! So I easily explained the glowing phosphorous by the fact that we messed up our own trail and one of us may have crossed the fence first and might have stepped on a earth worm or some kind of bug. The rest I assumed came from Fort Hood. I know of no pilot save the USCG helicopter guys or the Rangers that would even attempt that and I always wondered if they controlled that weather.

It was very odd. I am sure I could find that night on the weather reports!

It shouldn't be too hard to find a drop I calculated some where in the neighborhood of around of 150 million gallons of water/ sq. mi. in an hour! It took us a couple of days to find the 8' X 25' covert pipe which swished down two miles of water gaps and fence. Cattle died!

What I couldn't explain away, was the no sound, no air, no wind (not even from the clouds and weather). It was like the dead calm except for the raging River that tore out our covert pipe and sent all our hard work to the next county almost!! We were missing two hours of time also!"

I received the following e-mail from Osame Muhemed.
Date: Wednesday, 13 October, 2010, 3:24 AM.
E-mail: osame@inbox.com
It is hereby reproduced as it was received, word for word, and unedited.

"Hi, this happened to me when I was about 10 years old.
My village is in North of Iraq in palace named Kirbchana It was the village of shake qadir kesnazany.
At night 11/4/1982 about 10 o'clock I went to hunting small bird near the monition was far from the village I heard strange motion inside the grasses we had light, I direct the light to see what it is!! I saw creature very near human but was not human because had big head and small body 2 big eyes.

It want to see me but the strange thing was its hand was exactly like human but long and was very nice I think was dressed, dress color was brown. I was confused and we run away to village ,we told what happened to my uncle ,the villagers went to the place they saw the grasses was broken but they did not find the creature just they saw Footprints of four creature. We did not saw the UFO. It is true and real. Thank you." Osame

I received the following e-mail from Coyote.
Date: Friday 15, October, 2010, at 2:20 PM
E-mail: koyoteboy76@yahoo.com
It is hereby reproduced as it was received, word for word, and unedited.
My abduction (Orange sphere). I am now 33 and the time of this event happened when I was 20 but have been afraid to talk about it due to the idea that maybe I was crazy or that no one would believe me I have only told my wife in more recent years.
This happened in the fall of 1996
I was 20 years old and a friend of mine and I had hitched hiked out to another friend of ours house who live outside Ferndale Montana as I didn't have a car at the time. It was fifteen miles from from Kalispell Montana.
It was an overcast evening in the early fall and by the time we got out to my friends house it was starting to get quite dark outside and as we walked up the dirt road in the woods we noticed that the dogs were not barking which was actually pretty odd as we could always here them bark as we approached the driveway. we kept walking up the road and Rob says to me "its too quite" thinking nothing of it kind of chuckled to myself saying "yeah" and lit a cigarette.
We walked up on the porch and just as I began to knock on the door I actually felt the hairs on the back of my neck stand up before that time I only thought this was a form of expression but its not this actually happened I stopped just before my hand made contact with the door.
And I looked over at Rob and Rob looked at me and I could see the expression on his face and knew instantly he felt the same way I was feeling.

93

At the same time we slowly turned around and there before us not anymore then 2 feet above the pine trees was a huge orange sphere glowing like molten metal as big as a house and completely silent!

I remember being so scared my nose began to tingle and I felt tears welling up in my eyes after that I must have zoned out for a long time I don't know exactly how long we hand been standing there 20 minutes?

An hour? Two hours?

I don't really know but I came out of what seemed to me like a trance like state and I no longer was smoking the cigarette I had lit was what seemed to be a few minutes before that, I had the lighter from my pocket and was holding it out towards this Orange Sphere flicking it I didn't even know I was doing it!

My friend Rob must have come to his senses just then too because at that same moment he grabbed my arm and says in a harsh whisper too me "KNOCK IT OFF!!"

I looked at Rob and could see the fear in his eyes he looked like he was going to cry and I felt the same I told him "we can't just stand here" and that we needed to find cover! Realizing our friend whom we came to see was not home and there was no place to go.

In the driveway was my friend old Subaru brat with no windows, we bolted for the car and each jumped in a door, Rob on the drivers side and me on the passengers side we sat there for a while and watched this thing which seemed to us to have a feeling of malevolence about it.

It sat there motionless for a long time and then through the overcast clouds we heard a small airplane thinking surly when it gets close enough it is gonna see this thing! As the plane got closer the Sphere seemed to shrink in size down to the size of a flashlight I though to myself how is that possible? As the plane passed out of site it seemed to just zip right back to its original size and I really studied it this time it was a solid object for sure!

I though to my self I could throw a rock and hit it and the noise that it would make would probably sound like a loud DONGG!

Like if I were to take a rock and throw it at a battleship was what I pictured in my head. It was solid! I could see it. I knew it wasn't a trick of the eye it was there!!

We watched it not knowing what to do or where to go for probably another 10 minutes right after this a huge beam of light came off it and hit the ground and started a sweeping motion back and forth as if it were looking for something at that point I was so scared I could barley move the feeling could only be described as horrifying as I realized something must be down here on the ground not far from us I said "Rob we gotta get inside that house!"

He looked at me and says to me "on the count of 3. 1.2.3 and we jumped out leaving the car doors open and bolted for the door with all my might I kicked the front door in and we bolted inside I took one of the kitchen chairs and propped it against the door handle.

I called the police in Kalispell first thing and told them my name and how old I was that I had not been drinking or doing drugs and that I wanted to report a U.F.O and would someone please come out here and see this thing, the police officer just laughed and said I can give you a 1-800 number to call and report U.F.Os if you would like?

I hung up the phone in frustration I was feeling pretty helpless and looking out the window could see that thing still out there like it was looking for something I'm guessing it must have been about 3 in the morning and was exhausted Rob and I both fell asleep on the kitchen floor.

When I woke up the sun was out and the was no sign of that thing out side but looking out the window and seeing the car doors still open gave me a very unsettling feeling about the events that happened just hours before.

I finally was able to track down my friend using his house phone and explaining to him what happened that night even now I don't think he trusts me about what happened as if maybe we were up to no good and trying to steal from him or something of that nature.

About a month after that I became obsessed with U.F.Os being a non-believer previously I was now fully obsessed.

My sleep patterns had changed I couldn't sleep at night almost out of fear and would stay up reading about U.F.O reports and abduction stories trying to weed out what was most likely a real one from someone just made up bullshit.

Then it happened one night I was laying in bed and had fallen a sleep when I recall waking up with these shadowy figures around my bed home alone and was terrified thinking this has got to be a dream but I knew it wasn't I was fully awake and I couldn't move I couldn't scream and then I don't recall what happened because I must have blacked out I woke up in my bed and it was morning. I told Rob about this and he looked at me once again with a terrified look and said "shut up I don't want to ever talk about this again!"

I've tried to get him to talk to me but he just wont at least not about that night or if he had the same experience with the so called "shadow people" I guess I will never know. I do know what happened to me was real."

Abel: Akkadian/Babylonian/Assyrian/Sumerian. Noun. Name.
Abel derived from the Anunnaki word "Abhal", "A-bel-alu". It is composed from three Ana'kh words:

1-A, which means: First; origin; sky.

2-Bel, which means: A creator god.

c-Alu, which means: The first created man-form with mental faculties.

Abel "Abhal", "A-bel-alu" the Anunnaki, became:

- Abhel in Hebrew (In primitive Hebrew: Hebel, Hebhel).
- Habeel in Arabic.
- Ablu in Akkadian and Sumerian. It was first mentioned in the legend of Tammuz (Ablu Kinu), and meant true son.
- Abel in several western languages.

The proto-Jewish Ab means source in Hebrew, and EL means God. The original Hebrew word is Hevel, meaning breath or vapor; it did not contain the words AB or EL.

In Ana'kh, we find a similar meaning, for the Anunnaki's Abel which means "original", and "first prototype", referring to the first intelligent Man on Earth.
A sect of Abelitae, who have lived in North Africa, mentioned Abel as Abil or Haabiil.
Epistemologically, Abel derived from the Assyrian Aplu or Ablu. It was first mentioned in the legend of Tammuz (Ablu Kinu), and meant true son. And the Assyrian word Ablu derived from the Anunnaki's word Abhal.
The Assyrian Aplu or Ablu, or Abal means son, and are similar to the Anunnaki's words Ibnu and Ibn, which also means son and/or the first created person. In Hebrew, it became Ben, and in Arabic, Ibn or Bin.

The genetic composition of Abel (Habeel), and how he fits in the Anunnaki-Bible equation:
In order to explain the genetic composition of Abel, an Ulema suggested that we should ask ourselves what kind of relation Eve and her children had with God and the Anunnaki. There is a vast literature about Eve, and lots of contradictory accounts about her true nature, her origin, her DNA, and above all, her relation to the Anunnaki, the Gods, and the Judeo-Christian-Muslim God.
Eve appeared in the Sumerian texts, in Phoenicians epics, in the Bible, in the Quran, in the Gnostics books, and in the Ulema's manuscripts. Eve story in the Bible is the less credible one. In some passages of the Sumerian texts, En.Ki as a king, a god and a creator, created Eve. However, according to other Sumerian texts and Anunnaki's mythology, it is not absolutely clear if En.Ki was the original and sole creator of Eve, because many other Sumerian deities participated in the creation of mankind, such as Angel Gabriel known as Gb'r, Inanna, to name a few.
Humans who were genetically created by the Anunnaki were produced from, and by a mixture of the DNA of an Anunnaki, usually a god or a goddess, and an earthy element. This element was described as either clay or specie of a primitive human being. The "genetic creation" of mankind was also produced by mixing Earth's clay and the blood of an Igigi god called Geshtu-e.

97

The intervention of an Anunnaki god was a prerequisite.

Thousands of years later, the Bible told us that Eve too received a divine help in the creation of her first two sons; they were fathered by the Lord not by Adam.

This could and would astonish the Christians.

Eve conceived Cain and Abel with the help of God. Only her third son Seth was the result of her union with Adam. And Seth came to life in Adam's likeness. So how did Cain and Abel look like? The Bible does not provide an answer.

From Genesis: 4:1 "...and she bore Cain saying: I have gotten a man with the help of the Lord. And again, she bore his brother Abel..."

Genesis 5:3: "When Adam had lived a hundred and thirty years, he became the father of a son in his own likeness, after his image, and named him Seth."

The Gnostics books shed a bright light on this situation; Cain was created by the Anunnaki god Enki, and a woman called KaVa, (Also Havvah and Hawwa) which is the original name of Eve in the ancient texts written thousands of years before the Bible was written and assembled.

This is the official version of the Gnostics. This means that Cain is not 100% human. Cain's blood is ¾ or ½ Anunnaki. The other two sons of Eve, Abel called "Hevel", and Seth called "Sata-Na-il" were less than ½ genetically Anunnaki, because they were the offspring of KaVa (Eve) and Ata.Bba (Original name of Adam).

Cain was superior to his brother Abel at so many levels, because he was the offspring of an Anunnaki.

Abel was inferior to Cain, because he was the offspring of an earthy element. The superiority of Cain was documented in the Bible, because the Bible (Old and New Testaments) clearly stated that Cain "rose far above Abel"!

Thus, the Ulema, conclude that:

- 1-Eve and Adam were not from the same race. Genetically, they were different.
- 2- The offspring people (First human race) of Eve were the result of a breeding by the Gods.

- 3-The children of Abel and Cain were genetically modified to fit the scenario of the Anunnaki.
- 4-The creation of the human race happened earlier, much earlier than the date suggested by Jewish, Christian and Muslim scriptures.
- 5-All human races came from the primordial female element: Eve.

Aberu: Container; tube. Aberu was used by the Anunnaki gods and goddesses, in their genetic laboratories to fashion the early forms of human beings.

Aberuchimiti: Laboratory tubes used in genetic creation.
It is composed of two words:
- **a**-Aberu, which means container; tube.
- **b**-Chimiti, which means a laboratory.
The word Chimiti appeared in Sumerian epics and texts.

Abi-Milki: Phoenician. Noun.
A contemporary of Pharaoh Akhenaten.
Abi-Milk ruled the Phoenician city of Tyre (Sour, today) during the reign of Pharaoh Akhenaten. Abi-Milki was also one of the authors of El Amarna Letters that mentioned many of the kings and rulers of the era, such as Etakkama of Kadesh Zimridi of Sidon (Saida, today), and Aziru of Amurru.
Abi-Milki corresponded regularly with Akhenaten, and in his letters, he reported on political situations in neighboring cities and towns in Phoenicia, Palestine and Syria.

Excerpt from his second letter to the pharaoh:
"...I have said to the sun-god (Akhenaten)
My lord, when shall I see the face of the King?
I am guarding Tyre (In Phoenicia)..."
Akhenaten who reigned about 3,500 years ago (The eighteenth dynasty) was the mentor of Moses, and other visionaries of the era.

99

Akhenaten abolished Egyptian polytheism, and established the worship of Aten, a single god, and represented Aten with the symbol of the Sun.

El Amarna Letters.

Pharaoh Akhenaten.

Abibaru: Ana'kh. Noun. Name for the flag and insignia of the Anunnaki. The Anunnaki's insignia is represented by:

- a-A cross;
- b-A triangle (Delta);
- c-A fish;
- d-A crescent;
- e-A disk;
- f-A winged disk;
- g-A rosette.

Abinadab: Hebrew. Noun.
There are several Biblical personages named Abinadab, but the one relating to the Anunnaki was a villager of Kiriath-jearim, and a member of the tribe of Judah. When the Philistines captured the Ark, it brought chaos everywhere they placed it.
The statue of their god Dagon was broken, people suddenly died, and altogether the Philistines realized that the Ark wished to be returned to the Israelites.
They took it to Abinadab, who was willing to accept it, knowing it for what it was an Anunnaki artifact that had to be carefully monitored and could be dangerous. No one was hurt in his house, and eventually he and his sons safely returned the Ark to Jerusalem, where David built a special warehouse for it.

Abiogenesis: A theory advancing the concept that under very specific conditions, life or organisms can develop spontaneously from non living molecules and precursors.
Thousands of years ago, the Anunnaki Ulema have said the very same thing; according to their book "Ilmu Al Dounia", "Even the universe and everything that has followed the creation of the universe came from Bilaya, or Faragh, which means the state of nothingness..."

Abiotic: Non biological in origin.

Abiroon: The name given by the Anunnaki to the Atlanteans.

It means "The people who crossed the lands or traversed sea and waters." Similar to "Habiru", the name given to the Hebrews.

Abkalu "Apkallu": Akkadian/Sumerian. Noun.
In Akkadian mythology, the Abkalu "Apkallu" were the seven (or sometimes eight) sages who served the Babylonian kings as vizirs (Ministers), advisors and guardians.
Some were poets, writers, historians and others were the scribes who wrote several Babylonian epics.

Abkalu "Apkallu" as Winged Genii/Angels.
The Griffin heads recall Ezekiel's notion of the Cherubim possessing an eagle's face.

These sages were:
1-Adapa (U-an, called Oannes),
2-U-an duga,
3-Eme-duga,
4-Enme-galama,

5-Enme-bulaga,
6-An-Enlida,
7-Utu-abzu.

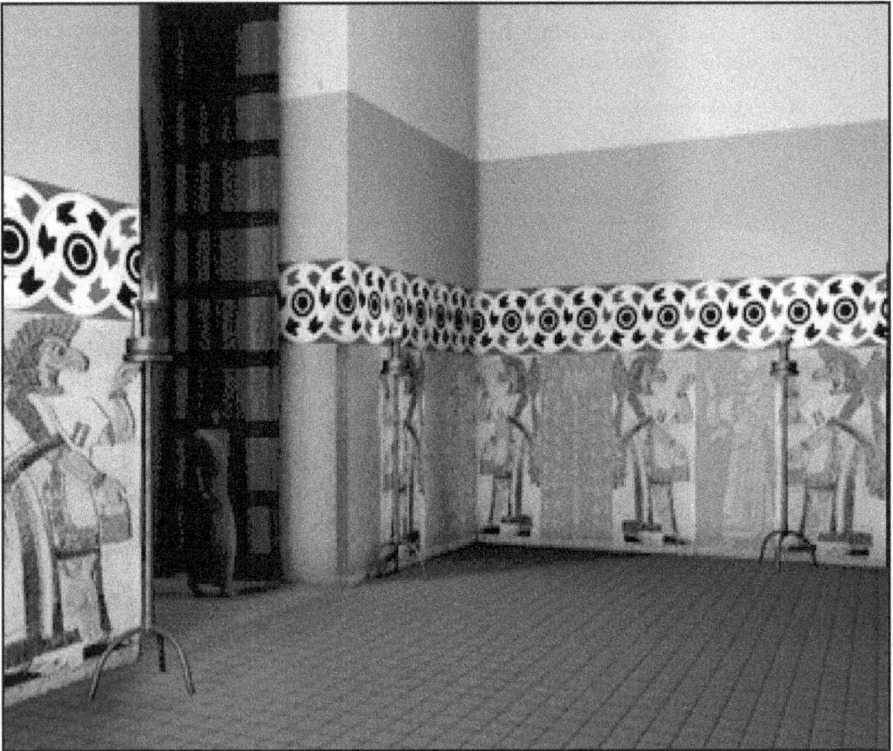

A room in the palace of Nimrud, decorated with Abkalu
"Apkallu".

King Ashurnasirpal (On the left) being protected from demons
and evil forces by Apkallu, his guardian spirit.

A typical Abkalu "Apkallu".

A Babylonian/Akkadian Abkalu guardian holding in his hand
Lagi-zulum (Spathe of the Male Date-Palm)

The goddess-angel Lama in a ritual gesture.
Photo: The goddess-angel Lama in a ritual gesture, circa 2330-
2150 B.C. Akkad period. Cylinder seal.
Mesopotamia.

Babylonian-Mesopotamian prayers had to be chanted or recited out loud and always accompanied by very specific ritual gestures, such as the "Su-ila", meaning, the "Uplifted hands."
These prayers were to be addressed to the Abkalu, who in return will elevate them to the gods. This seal depicts Lama, the angel-goddess praying in a ritual manner with uplifted hands.
This was the tradition observed during the Neo-Sumerian and Old Babylonian period, circa 2100-1600, B.C.

Several Babylonian deities were depicted as angels with or without wings. They acted as guardians (Abkalu), and protectors of worshipers, and in some instances, they offered their prayers to higher deities, on behalf of human beings.

The face of an Abkalu "Apkallu".

Slab from the Northwest Palace of Ashur-nasirpal II at Nimrud, 883-859 B.C, showing the king and his guardian angel, the

Ablu: Akkadian/Sumerian noun. It was first mentioned in the legend of Tammuz (Ablu Kinu), and meant true son. See Abel.

Abn'gal (Ab-ghal): Anunnaki/Sumerian/Akkadian. Noun.
Anunnaki name for the seven wise men who came from Apsu, the sweet water, and attended the gods of Enki.
They were known to the Sumerians/Babylonians as Abgal, and to the Akkadians as Akkallu. The Abn'gal taught the Phoenicians of the cities of Tyre and Sidon how to extract the Ourjouwan from the sea shells in the Mediterranean.
The Ab-n'gal had a small colony of extraterrestrials on the Island of Arwad.

Abradu: Name of the custodian of the conic books of an Anunnaki library, and particularly the calendars of future events. Usually depicted as a deity in the form of an eagle, or a man with the face of an eagle with large wings.
This depiction was very common in several manuscripts and calendars of the ancient world; Mesopotamia, Anatolia, Sumeria, Babylonia, Phoenicia, Turkey, Persia, and including the Mayas, Incas and Aztecs.
It is the belief of Ulema Mordachai ben Zvi, that there is a direct link between the remnants of the Anunnaki in Sumer and Phoenicia and the Pre-Columbian Mesoamerican civilizations.
The study of the Mayan calendar and other pertinent inscriptions revealed Mayan deities resembling the Abradus, and depicted as a man-eagle with huge wings. The Anunnaki calendar does not interpret time as a fixed period or periods or events, but rather a continuum of past/present/future. It is not linear but perpetual and shapeless.
Strikingly, the Mayan Trecenas share similar principle(s) and represent spiritual and non-linear concepts of time. In "Ilmu Donia" manuscripts, almost all the Abradus are depicted as a winged sage and/or an eagle with multiple wings, similar to the Mayan "Calendar Eagle", sometimes referred to as a dragon, or a celestial bird.

Absu "Abzu", "Ab-su": Sumerian/Akkadian. Noun.
Name of the temple of Enki. In the ancient Akkadian literature, temples were always Sumerian names.
Ea's temple in Eridu is called É-abzu.

111

The Pre-Columbian/Mayan Abradu on a Mesoamerican calendar

In Sumerian, É means house or temple

Absu is also the Sumerian limitless and endless space, out of which the first waters precipitated. This was where god Ab, the father of the waters and lord of knowledge lived. In the Anunnaki-Ulema tradition, Absu is the geneticist who fashioned the first "Liquid energy" on Earth.

According to the Babylonian Epic of Creation (Enuma Elish, "When on High") at first, there existed only the male (Apsu) and female (Tiamat) gods of the deep.

Apsu is a primeval Sumero-Akkadian god who personifies the primordial abyss of sweet waters underneath the earth. Apsu is the consort of Tiamat, the primordial abyss of salt waters of Chaos.

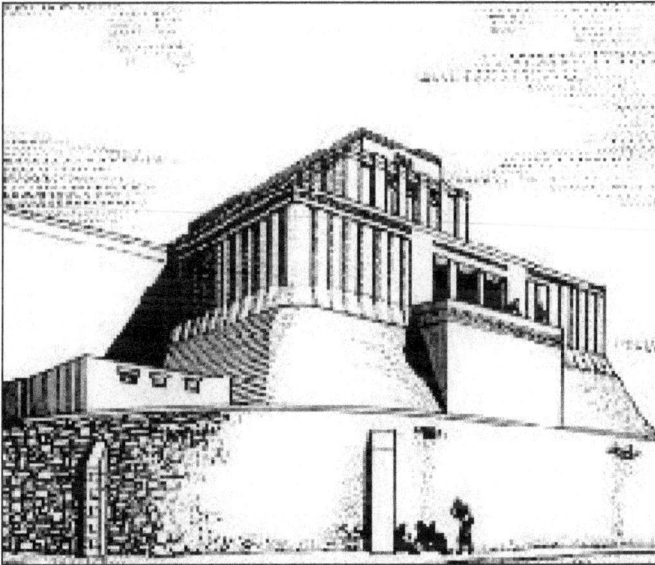

Enki's Temple of E.Abzu in the city of Eridu.

Enki in the Abzu (In the center).

Anunnaki god Ea (Right) in the Apsu.

114

"Apsû": Sumerian/Akkadian. Noun.
The subterranean waters, also known as the watery world of god Ea.
Abzu is the Sumerian limitless and endless space, out of which the first waters precipitated. This was where god Ab, the father of the waters and lord of knowledge lived.

Enki in the Abzu (In the center).

Abzu, Ea, Yahweh, the theme of water and "Tehom":
We learned from the Babylonian myths and poems that god Ea lives underneath Earth; a region that floats over the depot (Ocean) of fresh water, and which is found in the "Apzu", in the southern area of Babylon.
According to the Mesopotamians, that region was the source and origin of all the waters on Earth. And from that region emerged huge quantities of water in forms of streams.
This, made Ea (Enki) the lord (King) of waters, more precisely the "God of Waters" as described in the Mesopotamian clay tablets. The word Enki is in fact an attribute, a title, an adjective, because is it composed of 2 words:

115

a-"En", which means King or God.

b-"Ki", which means Earth, as well as the underworld, the underground, and the land of no return.

Ea sits over a throne of fresh waters. In the Phoenician and Ugaritic myths, Bull-El or El resides deep inside a mountain, referred to by the ancient scribes as "Tehom", which is the source of the fresh and the salt water of the oceans, exactly as mentioned in the Anunnaki-Sumerian texts!

Thus, the Phoenician god is closely associated with water, rivers and the sea, similar to Enki who lives in the watery depths of the Apzu, which also is the source of freshwater rivers and streams. In the Bible, Yahweh also sits on a throne of fresh waters.

The throne of Yahweh is placed on the top of stream of sweet and fresh waters, from the Temple in Jerusalem, all the way to the Dead Sea.

Yahweh, and Ea/Enki create a spring in the Garden of Eden:

From the Akkadian-Sumerian clay tablets we know that Ea "Enki" created a huge fountain (A pond, a lake, a river) in the garden of Idin (Eden). The Bible told us that Yahweh created a spring in the Garden of Eden (The same garden) which gave birth to four ancient rivers, called the Euphrates, the Hiddekel, the Pishon and the Gihon.

Numerous Mesopotamian slabs and seals depicted Ea "Enki" as an imposing god seated on a high throne with four or five streams of water (in the form of rivers) emanating from and/or around his shoulders.

One of the characteristics and attribute of Ea is "The God of water", frequently associated with "Apsu" which means in Sumero-Akkadian, ground-water.

Numerous Mesopotamian clay tablets depicted Ea "Enki" as a god inhabiting the "Apsu", and "Apsu" is where he dwells. As such, he is the universal creator, for water was needed to create the world. In the Koran, we find a reference made to Allah as the creator of the universe, because he created water. The Koran stated, "Wa Khalakna Lakoum min Al Ma'I, Koula Chay'en Hay", which means verbatim, "And we have created for you from the water each life-form (Or each living creature).

In the old-Babylonian epics, water played a paramount and primordial role; water gave birth to the world, and water through the Great Deluge destroyed the world.

Unforgettable historical figures in the Sumero-Akkadian epics were commonly and frequently associated with water, such as Pir-napishtim (Also called Utnapishtim, Ziusudra and Atrahasis) who became the Hebrew Noah. In fact, the Hebrew story of the Great Deluge is the same story of the old Babylonian Deluge, which is *de facto*, the flood of the Euphrates River.

Avraham ben Shmuel Abulafia.

Abulafia, Avraham ben Shmuel: Hebrew.
Name of an Anunnaki Ulema.
Abulafia was a Jewish mystic and Kabbalist. He was born in Saragossa, Spain, in 1240, and died in 1291 or shortly after.
A brilliant scholar, Abulafia developed his own version of prophetic Kabbalah and a sophisticated form of meditation.

117

He spent much of his life traveling in Europe, particularly Spain and Italy, and then the Middle East, including Israel, where he tried to find the legendary river Sambation and the lost Ten Tribes.

As an Anunnaki-Ulema, Abulafia was particularly interested in reconciling Judaism, Christianity and Islam, even attempting to convince the Pope (Nicholas III) to help the Jews. The pope sentenced him to be burned at the stake, but by coincidence that was later proclaimed as a miracle, died from a heart attack on the day Abulafia was supposed to be killed. Abulafia was therefore freed. After more travel, he settled in a small island near Malta, where he wrote most of his books, including the famous *Sefer Ha'Ot* (Book of the Sign) and *Imrei Shefer* (Words of Beauty). Abulafia is considered one of the most important founders of the Spanish Kabbalah. Some say he declared himself the Messiah. Others claim that he was strongly influenced by Sufism and Buddhism. All these misconception are derived from his secret association with the Anunnaki-Ulema, which he never fully revealed. From the book Who's who in theAnunnaki World, co-authored by de Lafayette and dr. Anbel.

ACAMSD: Acronym for the United States Aerospace, Chemical and Material Sciences Directorate, which for many years studied various space anomalies and their possible link to UFOs.

Accretion: A cosmic process by which small particles in the cosmos collide against each other, and stick all together to create larger celestial objects; an immense circumstellar disk of matter, which includes cosmic dust and gas, called protoplanetary ring or disk.

ACOM: Acronym for alien communications. See Aliens.

Adaam: Akkadian. Noun. The name of Adam.
Aadam in Arabic.
Aw-Dawm in Hebrew.
Adm in Ugaritic.
Adm' in Phoenician, according to the Script of Byblos.

Adama "Adamah" in Sumerian, Akkadian, Old Babylonian and Chaldean.

Adamu and Adapa in Sumerian and Akkadian, as they appeared in the Sumero-Akkadian epics.

Adama as Adam was not a single person. He belonged to a group known as Adamah, "Those who are of the ground"; a tribe of human beings called Adamites as mentioned in Genesis 5:2.

From Adamah, derived the Hebrew word Aw-Dawm (Adam). "Male and female created He them, and blessed them and called their name Adam, in the day when they were created."- Genesis 5:2.

Adad: Proto-Sumerian/Akkadian/Phoenician. Noun.

An Assyrian governor standing before the deities Adad (centre) and Ishtar (left), limestone relief from Babylon, 8th century B.C.

As the son of the great Anunnaki god Anu, Adad became the Anunnaki-Akkadian supreme god of rain and storms. Adad has been identified with the Sumerian deity Ishkur. Adad was highly feared and revered in the northern part of Mesopotamia, and was often depicted as a powerful god holding sparkles of lighting in his right hand, and an enormous axe in his left.

Adad was compared to the Canaanite god Hadad ('Adad).

In Phoenicia, Arwad, Amrit, Ugarit, Assyria, Babylonia, and Syria, Adad was regarded as the god of magical powers, healing, divination and oracles. His epithet read: "Adad bel birim", which means "Lord of divination."

As the son of the great Anunnaki god Anu, Adad became the Anunnaki-Akkadian supreme god of rain and storms.

Adad, Baal Cycle, and Yahweh fighting the dragon:
The Mesopotamian clay tablets told us a story of God Marduk who fought and slaughtered Tiamat the dragon, in order to rule over the world.

In the Phoenician-Ugaritic story of "Baal Cycle", the Phoenician god Baal-Hadad fought the Lotan "Tannin" (dragon), the seven headed serpent-dragon of the sea located at a close proximity to Ugarit and Israel.

The Phoenician-Ugaritic dragon story was very well-known to the Hebrews who shared their borders with Phoenicia.

In the Jewish Bible, Yahweh fought the sea's dragon Leviathan. Isaiah 27:1 "In that day Jehovah with his hard and great and strong sword will punish leviathan the swift serpent, and leviathan the crooked serpent; and he will slay the monster that is in the sea."

Psalm 74:12-14 "Yet God is my King of old, Working salvation in the midst of the earth. Thou didst divide the sea by thy strength: Thou brakest the heads of the sea-monsters in the waters. Thou brakest the heads of leviathan in pieces; Thou gavest him to be food to the people inhabiting the wilderness."

The book of Job describes in detail Yahweh's fight and the fire of the dragon.

Job 41: "Canst thou draw out leviathan with a fishhook? Or press down his tongue with a cord? Canst thou put a rope into his nose? Or pierce his jaw through with a hook? His sneezings flash forth light, and his eyes are like the eyelids of the morning.
Out of his mouth go burning torches, and sparks of fire leap forth. Out of his nostrils a smoke goeth, as of a boiling pot and burning rushes.
His breath kindleth coals, and a flame goeth forth from his mouth." Unquestionably, the Biblical story of Yahweh fighting the dragon is copied from the "Baal Cycle", an Ugaritic story of god Baa-Hadad who fought against Yam.
The 13th century B.C. myth (Story) of the Phoenician god Baal-Hadad told us that he fought his brother Yam, also called Nahar, to dominate Earth and to rule over the whole world, while the Jewish story was written in 586 B.C.

*** *** ***

Adad

Baal-Adad
Baal-Adad, the Phoenician god of storms. From a stela found at
Bethsaida, Samaria, Israel.

(Note: Some historians have claimed that the Biblical story was written between 588 and 1200 B.C.)

The Biblical story of the Hebrew God Yahweh fighting Baal-Hadad is simply a reproduction of chapter two of the Ugaritic myth of Yaw (Yahweh) fighting against Baal for the domination of Earth. And the Phoenician dragon mythical story resurfaced once again in the New Testament.

Revelation 13:1 "...and he stood upon the sand of the sea. And I saw a beast coming up out of the sea, having ten horns, and seven heads, and on his horns ten diadems, and upon his heads names of blasphemy."-100 CE.

Many of the early Israelites saw Yahweh as a subordinate to the Phoenician god El. And thus, they equated him with Baal, the Canaanite god they worshiped, and whose attributes were given to Yahweh.

Yahweh was depicted as a storm-god who ruled over the waters. And Baal too, was a storm-god who conquered and dominated the waters, symbolized by a sea serpent and a sea-dragon.

The Psalms described Yahweh conquering and subduing the waters by destroying Rab and Leviathan the dragons, exactly as did the Phoenician God Baal who conquered the waters and destroyed the "Tanin", the sea-dragon.

Thus, it is obvious that the Story of Yahweh fighting the dragon originated from the Phoenician story of Baal fighting the dragon

The Cycle of Baal:

The Bible portrays Yahweh as the father of mankind. But centuries before the Hebrews "discovered" God, the Phoenicians called their god "El" (Also Baal-Hadad) the father of mankind, and his adjective was Ab-Adm.

In Ugaritic and Phoenician languages, Ab means father (Same as in Arabic and in so many Semite languages).

Adm means man, and linguistically, the word referred to Adam.

In Sumerian and Akkadian, Adam is called Adamu, a word found in the Mesopotamian myths and literature, centuries before the Hebrew Bible mentioned this word.

Baal of Ugarit.

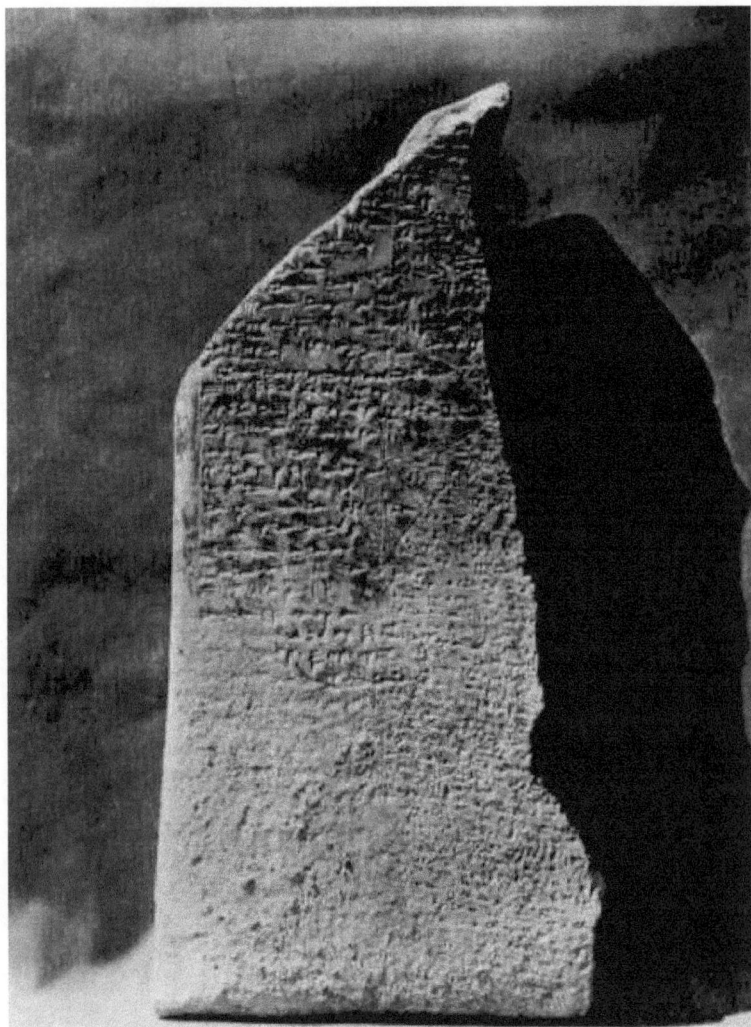

The slab of Baal.

Ironically or coincidentally, the Hebrew word Elohim (Name of the Hebrew God in a plural form) derived from the Ugaritic and Phoenician word "El".

It is historically and linguistically proven that the Phoenician god "EL" was the supreme god for both the early Israelites (Hebrews, Habiru) and the Phoenicians. In the Phoenician poem "The Cycle of Baal", El is called the supreme god, the creator and divider of lands, and Yaw is recognized as the son of El.

In the Cycle of Baal, as well as on the slab of Adoon (Adon, Adonis) we read verbatim: "El (Baal) is the supreme god, creator of nations, and Yaw is the name of my son...El, father of mankind and creator of the world..."

In Deuteronomy, 32:8, Yahweh appears to be a subordinate to El, and tells us that El-Elyon divided the world (Nations, countries, lands) between his sons, and the Hebrew Yahweh got the land of Israel as his share. Some scholars disagree.

They claim that Yahweh was first worshiped by the early Israelites in Edom. But this claim goes again common sense, historical veracity and recent archaeological findings.

Adama "Adamah": Sumerian/Akkadian/Chaldean. Noun.
Name of the first created humans on earth by god Enki and the Anunnaki goddesses.

Adama as Adam was not a single person. He belonged to a group known as Adamah, "Those who are of the ground"; a tribe of human beings called Adamites as mentioned in Genesis 5:2.

From Adamah, derived the Hebrew word Aw-Dawm (Adam).

"Male and Female created he them, and blessed them and called Their name Adam, in the day when they were created."- Genesis 5:2.

Adamu "Adapa": Sumerian/Babylonian. Noun.
Name of the first man who has lived on earth, according to the Sumerian and Babylonian mythologies. He was created by God Enki, sometimes Ea appears to be the creator.

From Adamu, derived the Arabic and Hebrew word Adam for "man", and Adamah, a Hebrew word signifying dust and earth, and in Aramaic signifying blood.

127

Ea created Adamu from clay found in abundance in Iraq (Sumer, Babylon in Mesopotamia). According to the Akkadian tablets, Adapa was the son of Ea, the creator-god f Eridu. Adapa learned how to write and how to read from Ea.

Legend has it that Adapa created the first spoken and written human language on Earth.

Adapa visited many nations and taught humanity, art, science, and the secrets of writing. The Babylonian scriptures described Adapa was one of the sages and citizens of Eridu.

The Akkadian/Sumerian clay tablets depicted him as a personage of a great wisdom.

Statue of Adapa, the Sage.

Adat "Adatt": Ana'kh/Hebrew noun.
In Ana'kh, Adatt means a reunion and a community.
It was the name given to the Anunnaki "Women of Lights" who were quarantined in the Arab Peninsula.
They were called "B'nat Nour", by the early inhabitants of the area. The words B'nat, Banat, Bint, Bintu mean daughter or girl, and they appeared in Hebrew, Aramaic, Arabic, Assyrian and proto-Sumerian. The word "Nour" means light in Ana'kh and Arabic.
In Hebrew, Adat means community; congregation. Derived from the Ana'kh Adaat or Adatt.

Addu "Addur", "Addursham":
Assyrian/Babylonian/Anunnaki. Noun.
Addu was also called Hadad. He was worshipped by the early Phoenicians, and was known to the Babylonians and Assyrians as Rammanu Rimmon "The thunderer King". In the Deluge story from the Epic of Gilgamesh, he was mentioned as the mighty god of thunder. Addu is also identified as Merodach, the god of rain.
His attributes were taken from the epithet of the Anunnaki's Sinhar Addur, also called Addursham. In Ana'kh, Addur means capable, effective, mighty. And Sham, Shama, mean the sun.

Adon "Adonis": Phoenician/Greek. Noun.
The name of a Phoenician god. He was called Adonis by the Greeks, and Adonai by Semites and the Hebrews. Adonai is also the Hebrew name or expression for "My Master" or "My Lord".
In their prayer, the Jews pronounce Yahweh (YHWH) as Adonai. Yahweh was also called Adoni by the Hebrews.
Adonai is directly derived from the Phoenician words: "Adon" and "Adoon".
The Hebrew, Syriac, Aramaic and Arab words: "Eloi", "Elohak", "Eloh", "Elahona", "Elohaino", "Eli", "Elah" and "Allah" are derived from the Phoenician "El", which means God.
Adon was also called El.

An in-depth analysis of the ancient Sumerian tablets recorded in cuneiform and including the Atra Hasis, the Enuma Elish, Adafa, the Descent of Ishtar to the underworld, Tammuz and Ishtar, the Gilgamesh Epics, and Etana to name a few, revealed that Adonis was also an Anunnaki god.

Adonis (Adon) and Venus, by Titian, 1555.

Adonis was also identified with the Babylonian god Tammuz. The name Tammuz can be found in the ancient tablets "Tammuz and Ishtar", and in the Old Testament in Ezekiel 8:14. Tammuz was known to the Babylonians as Dumuzi.

Originally, Tammuz was depicted as one of the Elohim found in the ancient tablets of the Atra Hasis and the Enuma Elish. Worth mentioning here, that Elohim in this context refer to one of the names of the Anunnaki, the extraterrestrial gods.

In Sumerian, Tammuz means the "Sprout forth as a faithful son." According to Babylonian-Phoenician legends, as an Anunnaki king, Adonis, "Adon", "Adonai" appeared before Abraham and commanded him to lead his Ram "People" toward the promised land, Palestine. Later on, his name Adonis or Adon was associated with his new Hebrew name Adonai. And once again, he appeared before Moses as Adonai.

Adonis, dying and resurrecting Semitic God: Etruscan statue of Adonis, Semitic God that dies and resurrects every year.

From Exodus 4:10: "And Moses said to Yahweh Adonai: "Oh my Yahweh, I am not eloquent, neither heretofore, nor since thou has spoken unto thy servant, but I am slow of speech, and of a slow tongue." According to Phoenician mythology, Adonis was killed by the tusk of the wild boar. Following his death, the river "Nahr Ibrahim" located in Phoenicia (Modern day Lebanon) turned into a river of blood.

The Piazza Pancali, at the entry of Ortigia, included a temple dedicated to the Phoenician god Adonis.
The ruins were discovered in 1860 under old Spanish barracks.

Tammuz

Tammuz, "Dumuzi", "Adon" and Ishtar (Sumerian Inanna).

The Sumerian King List mentions two Dumuzis, one as the shepherd, who eventually became a king, and the other as a fisher, who reigned over Uruk.

Because of the paramount importance of agriculture in the Near East/Middle East (Mesopotamia, Syria and Phoenicia), especially in the 4th Millennium B.C., Tammuz, Tummuz, Adon, Adonis, and Dumuzi were considered the same deity.

Ruins of the temple of Adonis at Afka, Lebanon (Ancient Phoenicia).

In Mesopotamian and Babylonian mythologies, Dumuzi is the consort of Inanna who has been identified and/or associated with the Phoenician goddess Ishtar (Ashtaroot), the lover of Adon in the Phoenician mythology.

135

The Habiru (Hebrews), the Phoenicians and the Sumerians wrote about gods descending on earth to fertilize the earth, and fertilize women of the earth, thus giving birth to a new breed of humans. In addition to the Akkadian/Sumerian tablets, a

Phoenician tablet discovered in 1936 in Lebanon, described Adonis as a traveling young handsome god who descended on earth aboard a circular disc resembling the sun to fertilize the earth.

The ancient Phoenician and Sumerian tablets found in Sumer, Amrit, Ugarit and Byblos clearly identified Adon "Tammuz" as an extraterrestrial Anunnaki god.

The remains of a niched wall in Uruk.

This scene shows Dumuzi being captured at his sheepfold in the Sumerian Edin and bound by the serpent-like Ugalla demons who carry him off to the underworld.

Adan, Jannat: Arabic. Noun. The Garden of Eden.
Gan Eden in Hebrew.
"Jannat" means both a garden and the paradise in Arabic.
Ganta "Gentaa" in Aramaic and Assyrian means a garden.
Gentaa Edeen in Aramaic, Assyrian, Chaldean and Syriac, means the Garden of Eden.
The archaic proto-Aramaic words "Ganta", and "Genyaa" mean gardens.
From Genyaa, derived the Hebrew word Gan (A garden), and the Arabic words Genna, Jannah, and Gannah, which mean paradise (Fardaws in Islamic Arabic). The Plural is: Gannat, Gennat.
The Aramaic word Genyaa, originally derived from the Assyrian word Gan, which means a land measurement of an acre and a ninth.
Synonyms for Jannat as a paradise in Arabic, Urdu, Turkish, and Azerbaijani:
Jannah in Arabic.

Cennet in Turkish. Derived from Arabic.
Cennet in Azerbaijani. Derived from Turkish.
Janat in Urdu. Derived from Arabic.
Synonym in Persian (Farsi), and Arabic:
Ferdaws in Persian (Farsi). Derived from Arabic.
Ferdaus in Arabic.
Synonyms for Adan (Eden) in Arabic, Persian (Farsi), Turkish, Azerbaijani, and Urdu:
Adan in Persian (Farsi). Derived from Arabic.
Aden in Turkish. Derived from Arabic.
Eden in Azerbaijani. Derived from Turkish.
Eden in Urdu. Derived from Arabic.
Adan in Arabic.
The word Adan "Eden" derived from the Sumero-Akkadian word "Idin", which means:
a-An elevated plain.
b-A steppe. More precisely a plain or a garden with an elevated hill.
The Sumerian Edin also refer to "Tseru" or "Seru" in the Epic of Gilgamesh.

Two major sources of inspiration for the Hebrew Bible's story of Garden of Eden are:
1-The Epic of Gilgamesh, which is the first story of the Garden of Eden (Idin in Sumero-Akkadian) ever told in recorded history.
2-The Phoenician story of the Creation, which described in detail the garden of Taautus, the Phoenician god, creator of mankind and the universe.
The pre-Biblical Idin (Eridug in Sumerian, and Eridu in Akkadian) is the prototype of the Genesis story of Garden of Eden, cradle of the most important concepts and ideologies in mankind history, such as:
1-The creation of man.
2-The reason for creating Man.
3-Adam and Eve.
4-The Temptation of Eve.
5-Man being deprived from attaining immortality.
6-Yahweh warning Adam not to eat the forbidden fruit.

7-Man being born naked and the reason for it, and so on,
These philosophical and religious themes appeared in the "Adapa
and the South Wind" myth.
According to Genesis: 2:15, "The Lord God took the man and put
him in the Garden of Eden to till it and keep it."

Adm: Phoenician/Ugaritic/Canaanite. Noun.
a-Mankind.
b-Man.
The name of biblical Adam; the first Man on Earth, according to
the Bible and Koran.
Synonyms in Turkish, Hebrew, Assyrian, Phoenician, Ugaritic,
Sumerian, Akkadian, and Old Babylonian:
Adem in Turkish.
Aw-Dawm in Hebrew.
Adm in Ugaritic.
Adam in Ugaritic.
Adam in Phoenician.
Adm' in Phoenician, according to the Script of Byblos.
Adama "Adamah" in Sumerian.
Adama "Adamah" in Akkadian.
Adama "Adamah" in Old Babylonian.
Adama "Adamah" in Chaldean.
Adama "Adamah" in Assyrian.
Adaam in Chaldean.
Adamu in Sumerian.
Adamu in Akkadian.
Adapa in Sumerian.
Adapa in Akkadian.
Adama as Adam was not a single person. He belonged to a group
known as Adamah, "Those who are of the ground"; a tribe of
human beings called Adamites as mentioned in Genesis 5:2.
From Adamah, derived the Hebrew word Aw-Dawm (Adam).
"Male and female created He them, and blessed them and called
their name Adam, in the day when they were created."- Genesis
5:2.

The Phoenician-Ugaritic word "Adm" which meant "mankind" was taken and transformed by the Hebrews into Aw-Dawm, to refer to the first man created by Yahweh.

Thus, the early Hebrew scribes began to use it as an eponym for mankind. The new Hebrew word "Adam" was already used by the Phoenicians, hundreds of years before the Israelites knew who Adam was, and before they learned about the nature and origin of mankind.

However, some linguists have suggested that from the Akkadian word Adamu, derived the Arabic word Aadam, and the Hebrew words Aw-Dawm/Adam for "man", and Adamah, a Hebrew word signifying dust and earth. (Not to confound it with the Aramaic, Syriac and Arabic words Adamah and Damu, which mean blood.

Advanced quantum/relativity propulsion workshop, 1994: A workshop sponsored and conducted by NASA, which began on May 16, 1994 and lasted two days, held at the Jet Propulsion Laboratory, in order to explore and examine faster than light travel and aliens' antigravity spacecrafts.

Aerobiology: The study of possible lifeforms on Mars.

Aerial Phenomena Group: A term briefly used to refer to analyses and studies of UFOs, which were part of the Blue Book Project, previously called Project Grudge. Said group was directly linked to the Condon Committee.

Aerial Phenomena Research Organization (APRO): An organization established in 1952 in Tucson, Arizona, by Coral Lorenzen and Jim Lorenzen for the purpose of investigating UFOs' signtings, and gathering pertinent data. The organization gathered distinguished scientists, and serious UFOS' researchers, such as Dr. James E. McDonald. Went out of business in 1988.

Aerospace Defense Command (ADC): Two weeks after the termination of the Project Blue Book, ADC became seriously and actively involved with UFOs' sightings, retrieving pertinent data,

and collecting information, statistics, and reports by other United States' intelligence agencies.
ADC's name changed to NORAD, North American Aerospace Defense Command.

Coral Lorenzen and Jim Lorenzen.

Aetherius Society: A bizarre group established in London in 1954 by a taxi driver named George King (1919-1997), who claimed that the extraterrestrials chose him as their delegate and ambassador on Earth.
The society claimed that Dr. George King "was contacted by an extraterrestrial intelligence known as "Aetherius" in 1954, and founded The Aetherius Society in 1955 to promote and act upon the wisdom of highly evolved intelligences from other planets who communicated with, and through, him for over 40 years."
King claimed that the extraterrestrials bestowed upon him the titles of bishop, Sir, and Doctor.

AFL 202-2: A reference made to the United States Air Force's memorandum number 200 section 2, which includes regulations forbidding military personel drom divulging information about UFOs' crashes.

AFL 202-2 also mentions a penalty of $10,000, and a ten year imprisonment imposed upon all those (military men) who reveal any information pertaining to retrieved/crashed aliens' crafts.

AFOSR: Acronym for the United States Air Force Office of Scientific Research, located at the Pentagon, and operating from Room 3112. In 1966, the AFOSR commissioned the University of Colorado to conduct an official inquiry of the UFOs phenomena under the leadership of Dr. Edward U. Condon.

Afqa "Afka": Phoenician/Lebanese.
Name of an ancient Phoenician town in Lebanon (55 km from Beirut) where Adon (Adonis) was killed while hunting. Afqa is known for the ruins of the temple of Aphrodite (Venus).
The ancient Afqa was one of the earliest Anunnaki colonies in the Near East. King Hiram, founder of the world's first Freemasons rites worshipped there.

In 1937, a semi-official French expedition found tablets written in an unknown language (back then), decorated with mysterious symbols and mini-illustrations.
Dr. Leroux interpreted parts of the inscriptions, and stated, "There is no doubt in my mind, that these inscriptions are of Ana'kh origin..."
Anunnaki-Ulema Bukhtiar stated that at one time in ancient history, Afqa was used by the remnants of the Anunnaki, as a healing center. He added, "A small river found in Afqa contained minerals not found on Earth. And I am wondering whether the early remnants of the Anunnaki had something to do with it, or simply, the Afqa's small river was used a purification center, for the Anunnaki's Liquid Light or Mah'rit."

The legendary cave of Afka.

Waterfall of Afka.

Afrit "Afreet": Arabic. Noun. A supernatural creature which belongs to one of the Jinns (Djinns) infernal categories, who live underground.
Ifrit in Turkish. Afriteh in Farsi. Afrit in Urdu.

An Islamic Afrit.

Agirim: First baked clay. Composed of two words:
- a-A, which means first;
- b-Girim, which means Clay.

From Agirim, the Sumerian, Babylonian, and Akkadian word Girim (Clay) is derived.
According to Ulemite scrolls and Akkadian/Sumerian cuneiform tablets, the Anunnaki used Girim to create the first Man.

Agra-bida: An Ulemite/Anunnaki term for genes.
More precisely, extraterrestrial genes.
According to the Anunnaki-Ulema "Book of Ramadosh", humans were created via Anunnaki genetic procedures, mixing their genes with the DNA of a very primitive human race.
In another section of the Book, references were made to the primordial role of certain acids in the human body.
These acids were essential for the development of our brains, said Anunnaki-Ulema W. Li.

Agra-rihal: Anunnaki/Ulemite. Term. (Progeria)
An Anunnaki/Ulemite medical term for the progeria disease found in the genes of humans and the Grays aliens.

Agusi: Assyrian. Noun. Name of an Anunnaki's remnant, and King of Arpad, modern Tel-Rfad, (north of Aleppo, Syria), and the father of Aramu, who was the first known king of Urartu, the ancient kingdom of Armenia.

Ahat "Aqhat": Anunnaki/Phoenician. Noun.
Ahat was a Phoenician hero, a descendant from the Anunnaki, and a gift from god El to King Daniel who adopted him as his son.
Ahat was given a celestial bow made out of circular horns.
Anat (A Syrian, Canaanite and Phoenician goddess of earth) was attracted to the bow, but Ahat refused to give her his bow.
She got mad, and sent her attendant Yatpan, to kill Ahat.

Ahat was killed, and his bow was lost during his struggle with Yaptan.

The gods became angry, cursed humans, and the supreme god Baal punished mankind by stopping the rains from falling on the lands of Phoenicia, thus creating a drought, and causing the crops to fail, and the stored grains to rot.

Ahat ascended to Ashtari and became a legion commander under his new Anunnaki's name "Aqhat", given to him by Sinhar Marduck.

Anat as Astarte.

Ain: Anunnaki/Ulemite/Arabic. Noun.
The higher class of the Anunnaki is ruled by Baalshalimroot, and his followers called the "Shtaroout-Hxall Ain", meaning the inhabitants of the house of knowledge, or "those who see clearly."

The word "Ain" was later adopted by the early inhabitants of the Arab Peninsula. "Ain" in Arabic means "eye".
In the secret teachings of Sufism, visions of Al Hallaj, and of the greatest poetess of Sufism, Rabiha' Al Adawi Yah, known also as "Ha Chi katou Al Houbb Al Ilahi" (The mistress of the divine love), and in the banned book Shams Al Maa'Ref Al Kubrah (Book of the Sun of the Great Knowledge), the word "eye" meant the ultimate knowledge, or wisdom from above. "Above" clearly indicates the heavens.
Later on, it was used to symbolize the justice of God or "God watching over us."
And much later in history, several organizations, secret societies, and cultures adopted the "eye" as an institutional symbol, and caused it to appear on many temples' pillars, bank notes, including the US Dollar, and the early Illuminati manuscripts.

Airship Flap of the 1896-1897 UFOs' sightings.
Even though, avalanches of pieces of evidence, hundreds upon hundreds of irrefutable documents, and mountains of historical and scientific findings which demonstrated without the shadow of a doubt, that the unidentified flying crafts and UFOs' sightings of 1896-1897 had nothing to do with aliens, and extraterrestrial flying saucers, ufologists and ufology's enthusiasts still believe that what flew over American cities during the Great Airship Flap were aliens' UFOs!
They are absolutely wrong!!

*** *** ***

148

Here is the full story:

The first sighting of a single luminous flying saucer occurred on October 26, 1896, in San Francisco, California, as reported by a local resident.

On November 1, 1896, a man reported seeing an airship over Bolinas Ridge.

On November 17, 1896, many local residents reported a huge bright light moving in the sky, and flying at an approximate altitude of 300-400 feet.

It was beaming some sort of a light coming from under its belly. Some witnesses, even stated, that they saw people inside a dome on the top of the airship.

It appeared to them as if they were directing the flying object.

On November 20, 1896, several flying objects in the sky of Oakland, California were seen by thousands of witnesses. Many witnesses reported seeing different kinds of crafts on the ground with crew repairing the airships.

For the next three days, more flying objects with a visible round cockpit with people inside were spotted in various parts of California. A businessman and a former attorney general of the State of California, who became extremely interested in these sightings, told the media and the public that those flying objects were airships invented by a man who works for General Marco, then the commander-in-chief of the national military forces in Cuba.

Many believed that the attorney general's story was a cover-up. Even back then, conspiracies and cover-ups seemed to be part of official procedures, but what is very distinct and different from nowadays cover-ups, is the fact that the 1896's cover-up was not of a military or a governmental nature, but rather of a secretive business and entrepreneurial nature, as investigative discoveries and findings would later suggest.

Many embellished stories and fabrications began to circulate, and some leading newspapers fueled the curiosity of the public.

Artist's illustration of an airship of the era. Published by the
Saint Paul Globe, Minnesota in 1897.
Many witnesses reported seeing such airships with highly visible
wings.

Artist's illustration of one of the airships that appeared over California, and published by the San Francisco Call newspaper, on November 22, 1896.

But everything changed, when the airships, all of a sudden began to appear all over the country by March 1897, and especially on April 1, 1897, when a huge luminous airship, thirty foot long, displayed an astonishing flight pattern in the sky of Kansas City, which was witnessed by thousands of people, and reported by the New York Sun newspaper on April 3, 1897.

***   ***   ***

Different shapes of flying objects:

One judge in Texas claimed that he spoke to a crew of a two hundred foot long airship who told him that they came from the North Pole and were en route around the world.
Several witnesses from Wisconsin, Iowa, Kansas, and California described the mystery airship as a long metallic cigar flying at a low altitude. While other witnesses stated that the airship was round like a balloon with a shiny metallic body. A third group reported that the airship had the shape of a cigar which lifted a rectangular compartment underneath.
The compartment which looked like a cabin was well-lit, and a crew of three people was seen inside the dome maneuvering the craft. The different versions of the shape, speed and altitude of the flying object led observers and concerned investigators to believe that there were more than one airship in the area, especially when latest sighting's reports described the object as a round airship with huge dome (cockpit) attached to two wings on both side of the airship.
It got more interesting, and perhaps more complicated when numerous witnesses reported that the crew of the airship was beaming some sort of light over houses and particular areas on the ground.

The varied versions of the description of the mysterious flying objects were published in the Chicago Tribune, the New York Sun, the Chicago Times, the New York Herald, and the New York Times.
The New York Times published 3 photos of the airship, and other newspapers sketched the flying object according to eye witnesses' reports.

*** *** ***

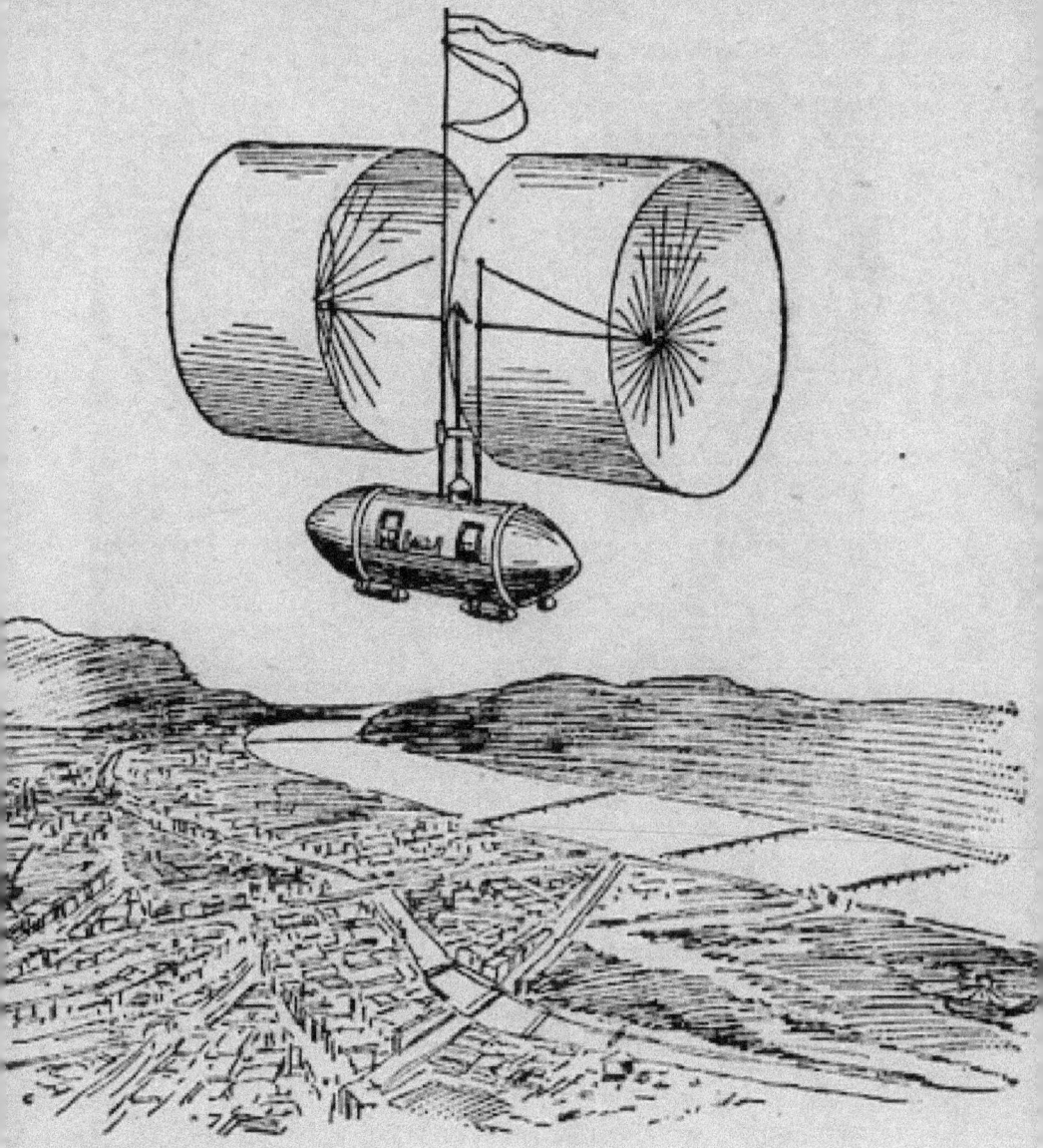

1897 Wellner's airship.

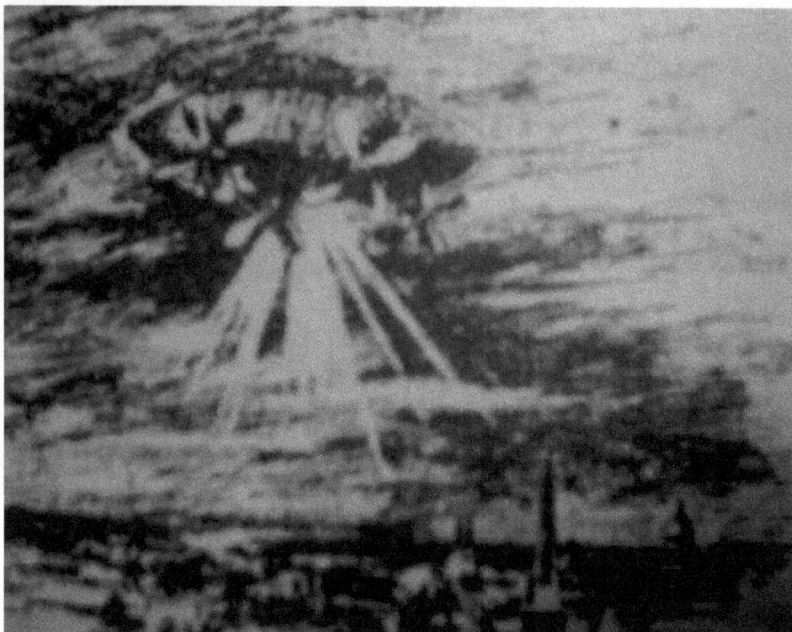

Airship over Sacramento, California, in 1896, as published by the San Francisco Call.

Articles in the papers of the era mentioned John W. Keely's airship which he built and kept on developing between 1888 and 1893. The airship flew successfully and was acknowledged by the United States War Department in 1896.

By now, everybody has heard of the mysterious flying objects.

Press clippings:
On April 12, 1897, the Chicago Tribune published the following, and contributed to Max L. Harmar, the Secretary of the Chicago Aeronautical Society, "One person knows all about the airship. He says: These thousands of people didn't see a steel hull because this is the airship my friend built in California and is on its way here to Chicago."

On April 2, 1897, the Chicago Record reported, "Missouri people excited: Mystical black object casting before it red light startled whole city for the last two weeks! Ten thousand people swear they have no hallucinations! Scoffers and disbelievers claim the people have been seeing the planet Venus or the Evening Star, even though according to the almanac this planet should have set below the horizon at least an hour before!

154

An artist illustration of an airship over Chicago published by the Chicago Times-Herald, on April 12, 1897.

Object appeared very swiftly, then appeared to stop and hover over the city for ten minutes at a time, then after flashing its green-blue and white lights, shot upwards into space....light gradually twinkling away and looking like a bright star."

On December 1, 1896, the Oakland Tribune newspaper reported that an airship was seen over Oakland, California, on November 26, and a witness described the object as a big black cigar...it was100 feet in length, and a triangular tail was attached to it.

It appeared that the main body of the airship was made of aluminum. It flew at a tremendous speed.

Deputy Sheriff John McLemore of Garland County, and Constable John Sumpter Jr. stated that on the night of May 6, 1897, they noticed a brilliant light in the sky, and later saw two persons moving around the airship carrying lanterns. One of the men approached them and told them that he and two other persons were traveling around the country in an airship.

Artist's illustration of one of the airships that appeared over California, and published by the Oakland Tribune and other San Francisco newspapers, in 1897.

The Deputy Sheriff and the Constable described the airship as a cigar-shaped airship, sixty feet in length, similar to those the newspapers wrote about.

On May 13, 1897, the Arkansas Weekly World paper wrote, a man was filling a sack with water and a woman was standing in the dark. The paper stated, word for word, "The man with the whiskers invited us to take a ride, saying that he could take us where it was not raining."

"We told him we preferred to get wet."

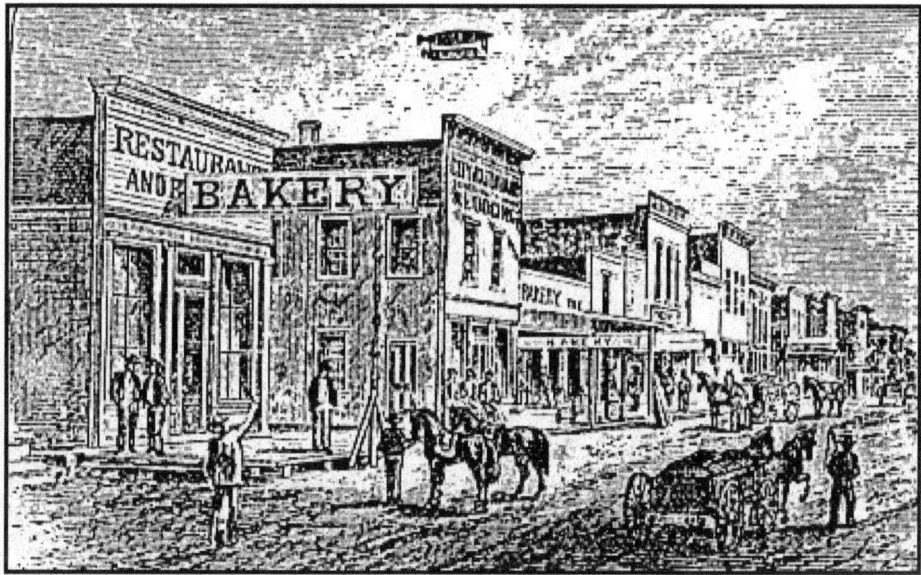

Artist's illustration of the era of an airship over Arkansas, 1897.

"Asking the man why the brilliant light was turned on and off so much, he replied that the light was so powerful that it consumed a great deal of his motive power. He said he would like to stop off in Hot Springs for a few days and take the hot baths, but his time was limited and he could not. He said they were going to wind up at Nashville, Tennessee, after thoroughly seeing the country."

On April 26, 1896, The Houston Daily Post, Merkel, Texas, published the following article: "Some parties returning from church last night noticed a heavy object dragging along with a rope attached. They followed it until in crossing the railroad it caught on a rail. On looking up they saw what they supposed was the airship. It was not near enough to get an idea of the dimensions.
A light could be seen protruding from several windows; one bright light in front like the headlight of a locomotive. After some ten minutes a man was seen descending the rope; he came near enough to be plainly seen.
He wore a light blue sailor suit, was small in size. He stopped when he discovered parties at the anchor and cut the ropes below him and sailed off in a northeast direction.

Artist's illustration of the mysterious airship of 1896-1897.

The anchor is now on exhibition at the blacksmith shop of Elliott and Miller and is attracting the attention of hundreds of people. Des Moines Leader, April 11, 1897, reported that the residents of Waterloo, Iowa, found a 36-foot airship made from wood and canvas and fitted with generators compressors. The airship was directed by a large crew. The "operators" of the craft told the residents of the area that they flew from San Francisco.

An airship landed in Iowa, 1987.

Testimonies and affidavits:

Alexander Hamilton, member of the House of Representative, E. W. Wharton, State Oil Inspector, M. E. H.unt, Sheriff, W. L.auber, Deputy Sheriff, H. H. Winter, Banker, H. S. Johnson, Pharmacist, J. H. Stitcher, Attorney, Alexander Stewart, Justice of the Peace, H. C. Rollins, Postmaster, and James W. Martin, Registrar of Deeds, signed an affidavit on April, 21, 1897, in which she stated (Excerpts), "We are awakened by a noise among the cattle.

I rose, thinking that perhaps my bulldog was performing some of his pranks, but upon going to the door saw to my utter astonishment an airship slowly descending upon my cow lot, about forty rods from the house...the ship had been gently descending until it was not more than thirty feet above the ground, and we came within fifty yards of it.

It consisted of a great cigar-shaped portion, possibly three hundred feet long, with a carriage underneath. The carriage was made of glass or some other transparent substance alternating with a narrow strip of some material. It was brilliantly lighted within and everything was plainly visible-it was occupied by six of the strangest beings I ever saw. They were jabbering together, but we could not understand a word they said.

Every part of the vessel which was not transparent was of dark reddish color. We stood mute with wonder and fright, when some noise attracted their attention and they turned a light directly upon us. Immediately on catching sight of us they turned on some unknown power, and a great turbine wheel, about thirty feet in diameter, which was slowly revolving below the craft began to buzz and the vessel rose lightly as a bird.

159

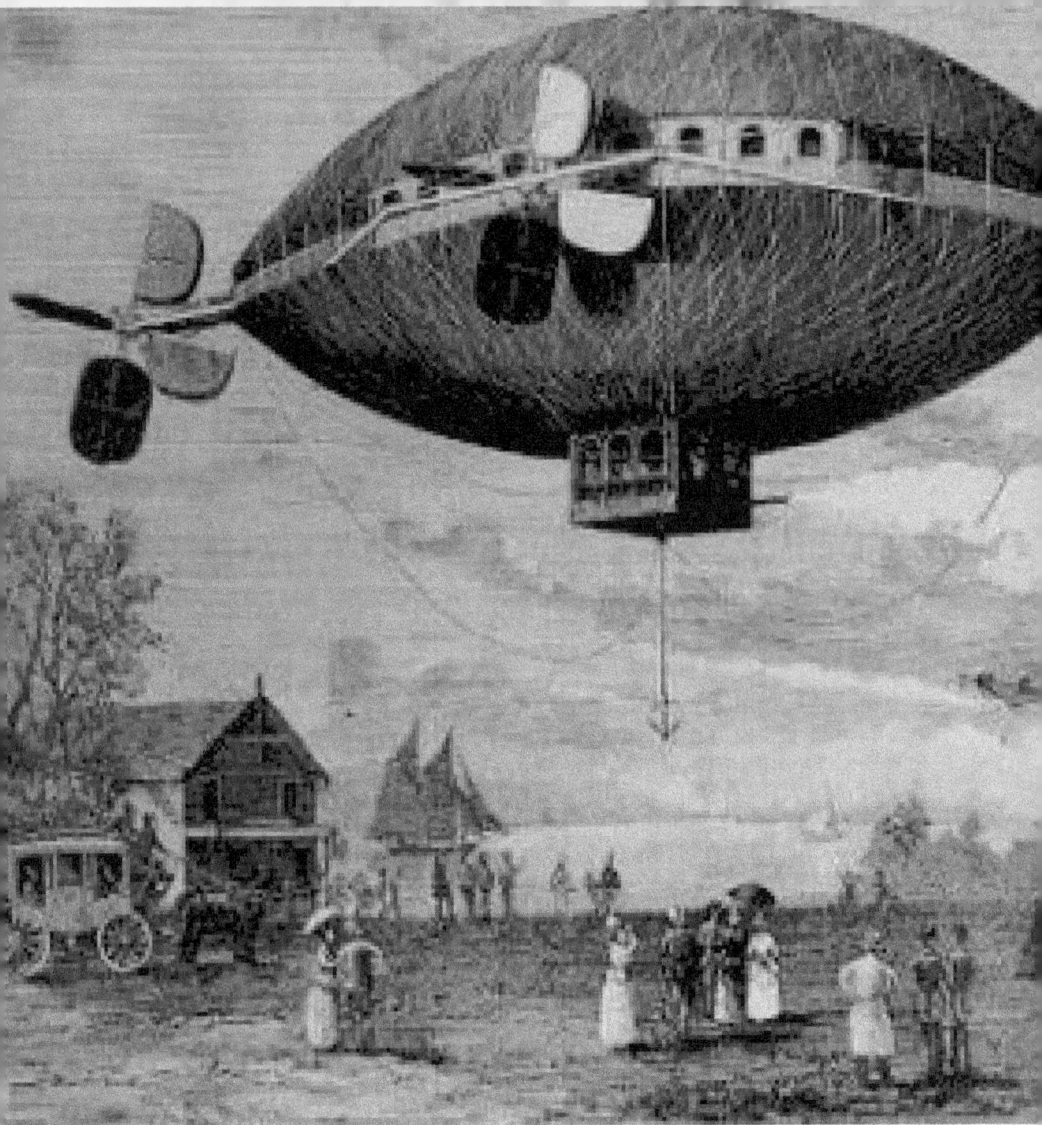

Era's illustration of an airship.

When about three hundred feet above us it seemed to pause and hover directly over a two year old heifer, which was bawling and jumping, apparently fast in the fence. Going to her, we found a cable about a half inch in thickness made of some red material, fastened in a slip knot around her neck, one end passing up to the vessel, and the heifer tangled in the wire fence.

We tried to get it off but could not, so we cut the wire loose and stood in amazement to see the ship, heifer and all, rise slowly, disappearing in the northwest.

We went home, but I saw so frightened I could not sleep. Rising early Tuesday, I started out by horse, hoping to find some trace of my cow. This I failed to do, but coming back in the evening found that Link Thomas, about three or four miles west of Le Roy, had found the hide, legs and head in the field that day. He, thinking someone had butchered a stolen beast, had brought the hide to town for identification, but was greatly mystified in not being able to find any tracks in the soft ground.

After identifying the hide by my brand, I went home. But every time I would drop to sleep I would see the cursed thing, with its big lights and hideous people.

I don't know whether they are devils or angles, or what; but we all saw them, and my whole family saw the ship, and I don't want any more to do with them."

The Great Airship Scare ended in April 1897 with the last sighting of an airship over Yonkers, New York.

No aliens, and nothing extraterrestrial here!

In conclusion, the airships were man-made, and had no relation whatsoever to extraterrestrials. They were built in Europe, and few were constructed in the United States, as documented by historical facts.

Many witnesses have reported that the airships made several landings, and their crew conversed with people, and asked for direction, supplies, and water for their crafts.

The crews were polite, spoke in perfect English, and were dressed very normally; nothing to indicate that they were aliens. Some explained why they were flying those crafts, what their destination was, and where they came from.

The majority would say that they were exploring the countryside. Others were more discreet and didn't say much. Nevertheless, they were humans, and from the United States.

The bottom line is this: All those airships were the earliest types and categories of dirigibles, motor-driven, and crews-manned crafts, and had nothing to do with extraterrestrial UFOs.

161

Yet, ufologists still insist that they are of an extraterrestrial origin and piloted by aliens!

Ufologists' false claims, accounts and explanations:
Ufologists have claimed that what people saw in the skies of 1896 and 1897 were extraterrestrial UFOs piloted by aliens. As usual they are wrong, and I am going to prove it to you. They argue that back then, no airship or any kind of a spacecraft was built, and/or was man-made in 1896 and 1897, simply because we did not have the technology of space-flight.

Little did they know that de facto in 1852, several types of crafts were built in Europe, and in 1894, 1895, 1896, and 1896, American entrepreneurs, businessmen and pilots began to build their own flying crafts, and kept them shrouded in secrecy, so competitors and business entrepreneurs would not know about it.

Several types of crafts were built in Europe:

In early 1852, French Henry Giffard built the world first three-horse-power steam engine airship; a mechanical flying machine. And on September 24 of 1852, Giffard flew his craft from Paris to Trappes at an approximate speed of 8 kilometers per hour, covering an approximate distance of 27 kilometers.

In 1853, Sir George Cayley created the world's first airplanes' model and flew an airship at a speed of 6 kilometers per hour.

In fact, in 1809, Sir Cayley wrote mathematical formulae for space powered flights, and established technical data pertaining to drag and thrust.

In 1872, German flyer Paul Haenlein flew his airship at a higher speed and at a higher altitude, and took Europe by storm.

In 1883, French engineers and pilots Gaston Tissandier and Albert Tissandier built the world first flying machine powered by an electric engine "Moteur Electrique".

In 1884, French Charles Renard and Arthur Krebs built and flew "La France", an airship powered with an electric motor at an approximate speed of 23 kilometers per hour.

In 1894, Australian Lawrence Hargrave invented a motorized kite-plane which lifted a load of 208 pounds.

In 1897, German engineer David Schwartz built a revolutionary airship powered with a gasoline engine.

In 1898, Brazilian-French aristocrat Alberto Santos-Dumont flew a gasoline-powered dirigible, (round-trip) from Saint Cloud to the Eiffel Tower.

Santos-Dumont was the world's first pilot-entrepreneur to charter regular passengers' flights with his airship called No.9 dirigible.

Austrian German Otto Lillienthal (See below), nicknamed "The "Birdman of Berlin" had to his credits over 2,000 flights, but unfortunately his illustrious career ended in 1896 with a fatal crash.

Lawrence Hargrave on Australia's $20 bill.

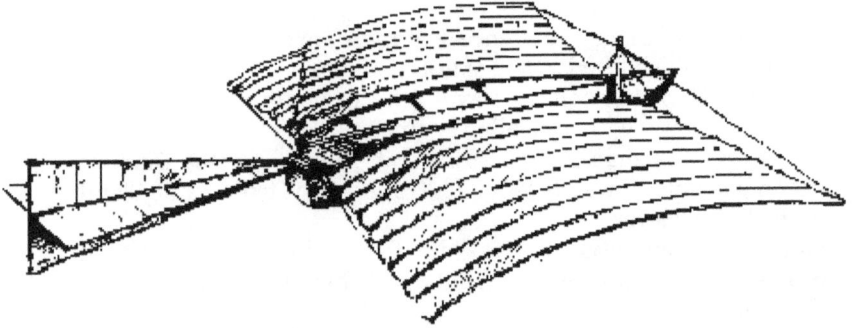

Sir George Cayley's first flying model, 1809.

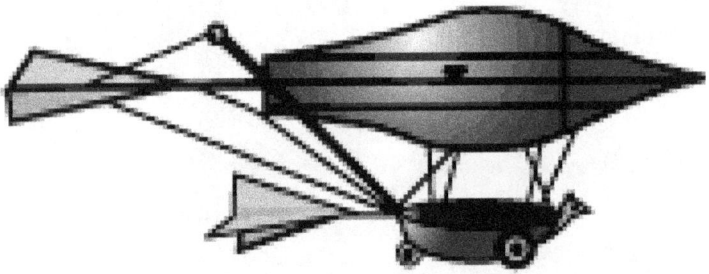

Sir George Cayley's first man-carrying glider, 1849.

Sir George Cayley's glider, 1848.

Henry Giffard's 144 foot long airship, launched on September 24, 1852.

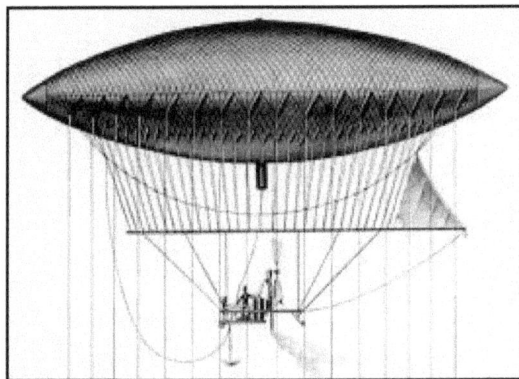

"La France" airship.

Arthur Krebs, co-builder of "La France" airship.

Alberto Santos-Dumont

Alberto
Dantos-Dumont's
airship around the
Eiffel Tower.

Alberto Dantos-Dumont's airship No. 9 over a French village.

Alberto Santos-Dumont dirigible airship.

French blueprints/patent of an airship design, 1852.

Count Ferdinand von Zeppelin's airship.

The ZR3

An all-metal airship built in 1897 by Serbian businessman and engineer David Schwarz, flew on November 3, 1897 over Berlin, Germany.

Engine of David Schwarz's airship.

Dr. H. Woelfert's airship, June 12, 1897, Germany.

Graf Zeppelin
mit dem Luftkreuzer „Z III" über Berlin

...-Aufnahme 1909
Ø 13.70/14

PHOTOCHEMIE, BERLIN N.

Zeppelin airship LZ III.

Various types of airships of the era.

Several types of airships were built in the United States. American inventors and builders of airships:

Do not underestimate the American entrepreneurial spirit!
During the American Civil War, Solomon Andrews built an airship and flew short distances.

- **In 1869,** British-American Frederick Marriott developed a model for transcontinental travel.
- **On July 2, 1869,** the 37-foot-long hydrogen filled balloon, "Avitor" powered with a steam engine and propellers mounted on its two wings flew, and became America's first controlled-flight aircraft.
- And at the San Francisco's Mechanics Fair, the "Avitor" flew 7 days a week, and transported thousands of spectators.
- **In 1889,** in Chicago, French-born Octave Chanute wrote "Progress in Flying Machines," which was considered back then as the world most authoritative aviation's technical reference and manual.

178

- **In 1891,** The Smithsonian Institution published "Experiments in Aerodynamics".
- **In 1895,** Cornell University granted Bachelor of Science degrees in aeronautics.
- **In 1895,** "The Aeronautical Annual" on flying machines was published.
- **On August 11, 1896,** Charles Abbot Smith received a patent number 565805 for his airship.
- **On April 20, 1897,** Henry Heintz received a patent number 580941 for his airship.
- **In 1896,** S.P. Langley flew two types of airships.
- **In 1896,** MIT began to offer courses in aeronautics and aviation, and MIT first degree in aeronautics was granted in 1892.
- **In 1896,** MIT built its first wind tunnel.

So, back then, in 1896 and 1897, we had the technology, the know-how, and the means that could have allowed us to fly. And there is no doubt that airships were built in America during those years.
But many pilots, inventors, businessmen, entrepreneurs and financiers of airplanes construction enterprises kept their inventions, airplanes and plans wrapped in secrecy for obvious reasons; business secrets and competition threats were two justifiable reasons for utmost secrecy.

*** *** ***

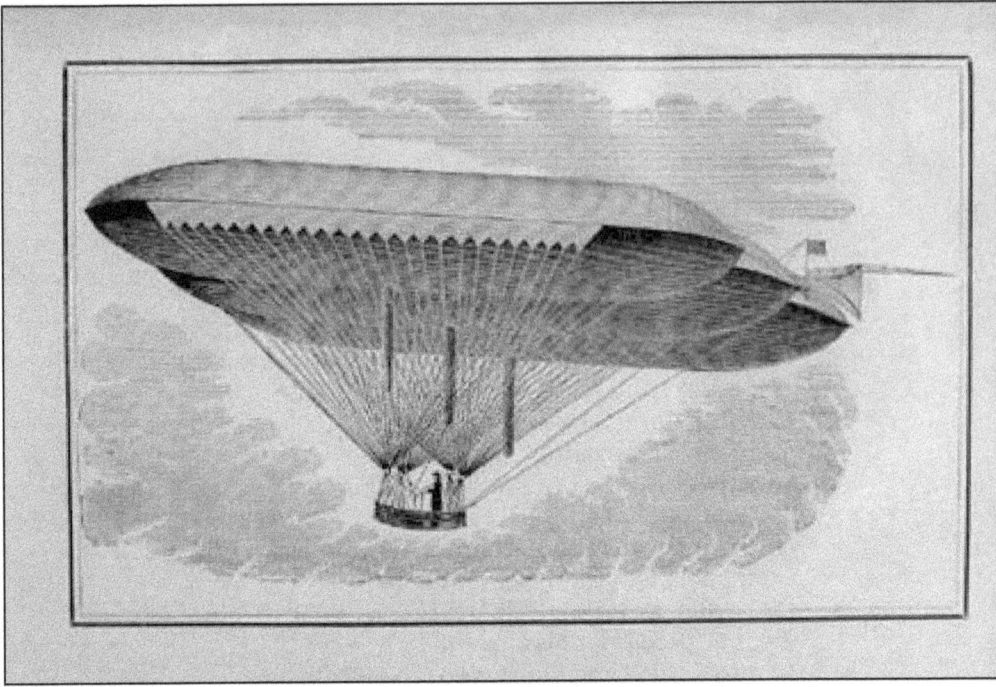

"Aereon", the First American dirigible "airship" built in 1863 by Solomon Andrews.

Solomon Andrews

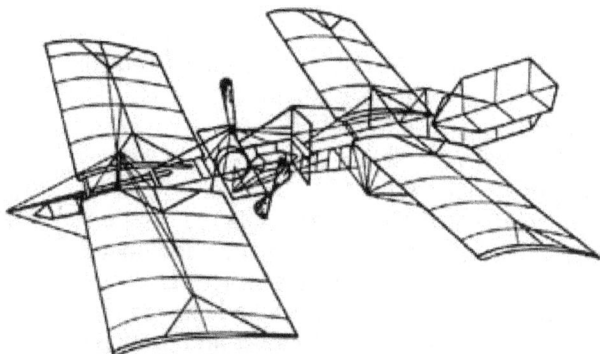

World's leading scientist in astrophysics, American Samuel
Pierpoint Langley's steam-powered aeroplane.
It flew half of a mile, and was witnessed by Alexander Graham
Bell.

Octave Chanute

Akashic Records Abhar:
I. Definition and introduction: What is Ab.har?
II. Ab.har and the Akashic Records
III. Description of the Akashic Records and the Anunnaki's
Akashic library

181

IV. The Anunnaki's library screen is contacted through the Conduit which is located in the brain's cells
V. Library's code of millions of years
VI.The Anunnaki's Miraya
VII. The Anunnaki's Minzar
VIII. By using one of the codes displayed on the Screen, you can hear the voice of Jesus, Mohammad, Napoleon, Socrates, Joan of Arc, or any humanity's greats' voice (s)
IX. Anunnaki can go back in time and change our DNA
X. Anunnaki can go back in the past and bring over people from other times

I. Definition and introduction: What is Ab.har?
An Anunnaki word for the Akashic Records maintained in the Anunnaki's library, also called the Akashic Library. The Akashic Library is really a very important part of the Anunnaki's culture.
The term Akashic is herewith used because many of us are familiar with what it means and represents.
The reason it is called the Akashic Library is because it has equipment that allows the researcher to connect to the Akashic Records; the vast compendium of knowledge encoded in a non-physical plane of existence, in a substance that is called Akasha. In Ana' kh, it is called Ab.Har, or simply Har.

II. Ab.har and the Akashic Records:
The Akashic Record has been described as a library, a universal computer, the mind of God, the universal mind, the collective wisdom, and a dozen other metaphors, but in the end it is a collection of records of everything that has ever been thought of or experienced, every word, every action. The individual records in the global Akashic Records are constantly updated.

III. Description of the Akashic Records and the Anunnaki's Akashic library:

The Ulema stated that on Adelbaran (Ashtari), each Anunnaki has access to the global Akashic Record through the Akashic libraries, which are located in every community.

Everywhere, the libraries have the same appearance, and they are built very differently from the normally classical architecture of the Anunnaki. Usually, the houses are built of various types of stone, marble, or bricks, but the libraries are constructed from materials such as glass, fibreglass, or other plastic-like materials; they give the impression of a modern, industrialized edifice.

One enters through a huge door that is never closed, day and night. It opens into a huge hall, seven hundred to one thousand meters in length, by five hundred meters in width.

The hall is empty of any furniture, and is lit by windows that are placed very high, near the ceiling. The windows were designed in such a way that the shafts of light that enter through them are very sharply delineated and look like solid beams of light. At night, the same effect is achieved by enormous spot lights placed near the windows.

The effect is incredibly effective. Extremely large billboards hang on each wall. On the floor in front of each billboard are hundreds of pads.

When visitors enter the library, they approach the billboard, stand each on a pad, and think about their destination within the building. The pad has the capacity to read minds, and as soon as it does so, it begins to move, and it slides right through the billboard, which is not really solid but is made of a form of energy, carrying the visitor with it. Behind the billboard is the main hall of the Akashic Library, called Mad-Khal.

IV. The Anunnaki's library screen is contacted through the Conduit which is located in the brain's cells:

The Anunnaki Akashic Library is not a library in the traditional sense, because it contains no physical books on shelves, and not even cones that are the normal format for an Anunnaki book.

Instead, the visitors find themselves in the presence of an immense screen, composed of a material not found on Earth. The screen is hard to describe; it can be compared to a grid, with a multitude of matrices and vortices of data.

183

The screen is contacted through the Conduit which is located in the brain's cells. The screen can read minds, and it knows right away what information the visitors seek.

All what the visitors have to do is stand still in front of the screen, and the data will be displayed in sequences. Of course, the data is not represented by lines, sentences, or paragraphs, but rather by codes.

V. Library's code of millions of years:
Each code contains particular information related to an aspect of the subject. For example, if you would like to visit Iraq, 2,000 A.D., Iraq 300 B.C., or Iraq 2,008 B.C., all you have to do is to focus on these dates, and three codes will appear on the screen waiting for your command to open them up.

From this moment on, the Conduit located in your brain and the screen are communicating in the most direct fashion. The three files (The nearest description of these files would be to call them digital, for the lack of the proper word) will open up. Each one will contain everything that had happened pertaining to that particular date in Iraq.

The Conduit will sort out, classify, and index the particular data for the part of the information the visitor is most interested in.

Then, the information will be stored automatically in the cells of the visitor's brain, increasing the size of the depot of knowledge in the brain.

And because Anunnaki are connected to each other and to their community via the Conduit, the data recently absorbed is sent to other Anunnaki to share it, which is extremely beneficial, since if the data received from the screen is difficult to understand, the Anunnaki community called Jama, or an individual Anunnaki, will send, also automatically, the explanation needed.

This is quite similar to an online technical support on earth, but it is much more efficient since it functions brain-to-brain. Each Anunnaki community have the same kind of center for these mirrors of knowledge which are the Akashic files. The complexity of the centers though, is not the same.

VI. The Anunnaki's Miraya: Some of the Akashic Libraries include more perplexing and complicated instruments and tools, which are not readily available to other communities.

These tools include the monitor, which is also called mirror or Miraya in Ana'kh. Each Miraya is under the direct control of a Sinhar (Anunnaki leader), who serves as custodian and guardian. It is very important to protect the privacy of every member of the community, because individual Anunnaki could attempt to tap into the data of the Miraya and have access to the codes of the telepathic communication of other Anunnaki, thus enabling them to read the mind of all the community members, something that is considered highly unethical and absolutely must be avoided.

The screens, by the way, can expand according to the number of codes that the Anunnaki researcher is using. Seven to ten codes are normal. If more codes than that are opened, the screen is fragmented into seven different screens, which are only visible to an Anunnaki mind. An amazing phenomenon occurs at this moment; time and space mingle together and become unified into one great continuum. This enables the researcher to grasp all the information in a fraction of a second.

An added convenient aspect of the Akashic files is the ability of the researcher to access them in the complete privacy of the researcher's home or office, since part the files can be teleported there.

VII. The Anunnaki's Minzar: But since the private screen is not as complicated as the central one in the Central Library, no multiple screen will open up, only the original one.

It is important to understand that the data received is not merely visual. There is much more to it than that. By the right side of the screen, there are metallic compartments as thin as parchment paper, which serve as a cosmic audio antennae, called Min-Zar.

These compartments search for, and bring back, any sound that occurred in history, in any era, in any country, and of any magnitude of importance; this includes voices of all kinds of people, including, saints, preachers, prophets, and wicked ones as well.

And this is just a minor part of it, because it brings additional sounds from other dimensions, and para-galactic civilizations (Terrestrials and extraterrestrials). According to the Anunnaki, every single sound or voice is never lost in the universe.
Of course, some sounds do not traverse certain boundaries. For humans, if the sound was produced on earth, such a boundary is the solar system.
Each of these antennae-compartments will probe different galaxies and star systems, listening, recording, retrieving, and playing back sounds, voices, and noises.

VIII. By using one of the codes displayed on the Screen, you can hear the voice of Jesus, Mohammad, Napoleon, Socrates, Joan of Arc, etc. "By using one of the codes displayed on the Screen, you can hear the voice of Jesus, Mohammad, Napoleon, Socrates, Joan of Arc, or any humanity's greats' voices," said Ulema Penjabi Tien Utan.
The voice is never lost, because it is energy and it stays in the perimeter of its sphere, call it for now, atmosphere, space, etc. The Anunnaki combined asset of the visual and audio systems provided by the Screen, gives anybody the ability to learn languages afforded by the Akashic Library. This applies to any language – past, present or future, and from any part of the universe. The researcher can call up a shining globe of light that will swirl on the screen with enormous speed. As it rotates, the effect blends with an audio transmission that comes from the metallic compartments.
In an instant, any language will sink into the brain's cells. On the left side of the screen, there are conic compartments that bring still images of certain important past events. This mini-screen-display informs the researcher that these particular events cannot be altered. In other words, the Anunnaki cannot go back in the past and change it. The Anunnaki are forbidden to change or alter the events, or even just parts or segments of past events represented on the conic compartment, because these images represent events created by the Anunnaki themselves.

IX. Anunnaki can go back in time and change our DNA:

This restriction works as a security device, an essential one.

For example, a young Anunnaki cannot visit planet Earth sixty five thousand years ago, enter the genetic lab of the Anunnaki in Sumer or Phoenicia, and change the DNA and the genetic formula originally used by Sinhar Enki, or Sinhar Anu, to create the human race, or the seven prototypes of the human race created by Sinhar Inanna.

Sinhar Inanna herself can go back and change it, but not for use on earth as we know it. She has to transpose it and transport it to another dimension, parallel to the original dimension where the event occurred. This safeguard means that Sinhar Inanna cannot recreate a new race on our earth by sending us, the current living humans, sixty five thousand years ago back in time, remoulding us, and then bringing us back to the twenty first century as new specie, or a new race.

This would be unethical. All she could do would be to recreate her own experiment in another dimension.

For instance, Inanna can go back 2,000 years in time and space, reconstruct the DNA of Jesus Christ and create a new Jesus. But the new Jesus will not exist on the map of year 1, or return to Bethlehem to be re-born again.

He will be transported as a grown man to another dimension not very much different from the Palestine Jesus knew. This almost crazy scenario does not contradict today's quantum physics. Scientifically and theoretically, it is possible.

Dr. Steven Hawking, as well as many of the brightest scientific minds of our time have accepted such possibilities.

The Anunnaki's Ba'ab, other universes, dimensions, and the creation of the future: Before the Anunnaki Screen, in the hall of the Akashic Records, more options are available for research, and one of them is a sort of browsing. Inside the screen, there is a slit where the mind of the Anunnaki can enter as a beam.

This will open the "Ba'abs", or Stargates, to other worlds that the researcher is not even aware of, but appeared randomly as part of the discovery or exploration.

In each slit there is another Akashic file that belongs to other universes, worlds, dimensions, and civilizations, sometimes more advanced than the Anunnaki themselves, where the researcher can either retrieve important information, and/or witness the creation of the future. It is like going back in the future, because everything present, or occurring in the future, has already occurred in a distant past and needed time to surface and appear before the current living Anunnaki. And there is also the aspect of simply having fun, some of it not so ethical.

X. Anunnaki can go back in the past and bring over people from other times: Sometimes an Anunnaki will go back in time, let's say 400 B.C., choose a famous historical figure, and at the same time bring over another important person, one thousand years older, simply to see how they would interact.
They can easily deceive these personages, since every Anunnaki is an adept at shape changing.
Or they can transpose people, move them in time, and see how they will react to the new environment.

For example, an Anunnaki can bring together John the Baptist, Hannibal, Charles Dickens and Marilyn Monroe and make them talk to each other. They might not relate to each other, but they will be brought again to one place chosen by the Anunnaki, and a real dialogue will take place. To many of us, this seems illogical, but to avant-garde astrophysicists, geneticists, and scientists this is a serious possibility.
To the Anunnaki, these extraordinary occurrences are games. These games are strictly forbidden, but some low class Anunnaki and undisciplined children sometime try it as amusement-game.
Sometimes they interfere with our daily affairs, and cause us temporary loss of memory as a result of that.
Anunnaki children, though usually extremely well-behaved, may also play silly games, such as deliberately misplacing our objects, our car keys, our cellular phone, pens, hats, and then returning them, to the amazement of the humans.
These tricks, while they can be quite annoying, never harm any one seriously. One unpleasant result may surface in therapy.

A psychiatrist might tell the person complaining of such an event that his or her mind is playing tricks. Well, it is indeed a trick, but not from the mind. It is performed by the Anunnaki people.

Akalicha "Akalikha": Anunnaki/Ulemite/Arabic. Noun.
The creation.
It is composed of two words:
a-An, which means origin; god; beginning;
b-Kalicha, which means the Creation.
The Anunnaki's creation of the world was briefly described in the Sumerian texts; only one account of the Sumerian creation has survived, but it is a suggestive one.
The creation account appeared as an introduction to the story of the Huluppu-Tree.

Akama-ra: Anunnaki/Ulemite. Noun. The Ulema said that the Akama-ra were the first beings who were allowed by Enki and Inanna to date the "Women of Light" who were quarantined on Earth by the Anunnaki. Akama-ra were genetically created by the Anunnaki on Ashtari and were transported to planet Earth on Anunnaki's spaceships, called Merkabah.

Akamu "Akama": Anunnaki/Ulemite/Assyrian. Noun.
In Assyrian, Akamu means gathering; assembly; group of people. Derived from the Ana'kh Akama. From Akamu, derived the Arabic word Kawmu, which means exactly the same thing.
According to Ulema Fadel Al Bakri Al Qaysi, the Akama were Anunnaki administrators who controlled the Akama-ra in quarantined areas in the Middle East. They established the rules of mating with the Anunnaki's Women of Light, also called "B'nat Nour".During their first interaction with Earth's quasi-humans, and later on with the humans they created, the Anunnaki did not want those species to mate or date with another category of beings they created from non-terrestrial genes.
Some of these extraterrestrial beings were created on Nibiru, and others in the Arab Peninsula. Among them were the Women of Lights as they were called by the inhabitants of the area.

The Akama were assigned the duty of supervising the Women of Light and the Akama-ra.

Akarta: Anunnaki word for celestial map, used as an almanach of stars by the early Babylonians, Akkadians, and Sumerians. Kharta in Arabic.

Babylonian astrology and astronomy tablet.
As translated from Akkadian Cuneiform, the tablet revealed a list of eclipses between 518 and 465. The tablet also mentioned and predicted the death of king Xeres. The tablet is on display at the British Museum. The Anunnaki taught the Babylonians science, arts, literature, and languages (Terrestrial and non-terrestrial languages mentioned in the Book of Ramadosh.)

The translation of this Babylonian tablet revealed what the Anunnaki taught the Babylonians astronomy, and how to map the "Heavens", a word for the known universe (Skies).
In fact, this Akkadian Cuneiform tablet is a Babylonian almanac, mentioning in detail, the future positions of the planets, some still unknown to us.

Ákaskala "Akashlala": Anunnaki/Sumerian. Noun.

191

In Sumerian, Ákaskala means plantation or fields' workers. It derived from the Anunnaki's word Akashlala, which refers to the humans created by the Anunnaki to replace the Igigi, who worked the fields of Sumer and fed the Anunnaki. The Akashlala were the first human beings workers who were created by the Anunnaki for that purpose. They were short, strong, and could lift extremely heavy loads of grains, cereals, and stones needed to fence the fields. However, they were deprived from developed mental faculties.

King Sargon

Akki: Akkadian/Sumerian. Noun.

Name of the good Anunnaki lord (disguised as a farmer and irrigator) who rescued King Sargon in his basket.

The Akkadian legend has it that Sargon's mother had set him floating on the Euphrates River. Akki found the little infant, rescued him, and raised him as his own son.

In the Bible, Moses, the little baby was found in a basket floating on the Nile River, and was rescued by an Egyptian princess. She raised him as her own son. Astonishing coincidence! Similarity or copiage?

Moses rescued from the Nile.

"And the woman conceived and bore a son; and when she saw that he was beautiful, she hid him for three months.
But when she could hide him no longer she got him a wicker basket and covered it over with tar and pitch. Then she put the child into it, and set it among the reeds by the bank of the Nile."
Exodus 2:2,3

Akurgal: Akkadian. Noun. An Anunnaki's offspring.
Akurgal was the king of Lagash and the father of Eannadu. Akurgal was the son of Ur-Nina. He defeated Ush of Umma and became King of Sumer and Akkad.

Al-Kaslik, Monastery of:

Monastery of Saint Antoine, Qozhaya, Lebanon.

A Christian Maronite monastery in Lebanon, custodian of vital and secret documents on the Gnostic Christianity, the Anunnaki and origin of man. The vaults of the monastery of Al Kaslik, and the Monastery of Saint Antoine, in Qozhaya, Lebanon, contains documents written in Ana'kh, the language of the Anunnaki.

194

Alaahaa: Syriac/Aramaic. Noun. God.
Synonyms in Ugaritic, Phoenician, Babylonian Assyrian, Arabic, Turkish, Urdu, Aramaic, Syriac, Azerbaijani, Chaldean, Akkadian, Persian (Farsi), and Hebrew:
Alaahaa in Chaldean.
Allah in Arabic.
Allah in Farsi.
Allah in Turkish.
Allah in Urdu.
Allah in Azerbaijani.
Yaw in Ugaritic.
Yaw in Phoenician.
Ya'u in Assyro-Babylonian.
Yehaw in Ugaritic.
Yehaw in Phoenician.
Yehi in Phoenician.
Yehi in Ugaritic.
Yehu in Ugaritic.
Yehu in Phoenician.
Yahweh in Hebrew.
Baal-El in Ugaritic.
Baal-El in Phoenician.
El (Eli, my god) in Aramaic.
Elo (Eloi, my god) in ancient Aramaic.
El (Eli, my god, my lord) in Chaldean.
Ilum in Akkadian.
Ilah in Arabic.
Ilahi (my god), in Arabic.
Rab in Assyrian.
Rabu in Assyrian.
Rabi in Assyrian.
Rab in Arabic.
Rab in Syriac.
Rab in Aramaic.
Rab in Chaldean.

Allah (Allahu, Ilah) is a Christian Arabic word adopted by the Prophet Mohammad, the Koran, the Islamic religion, and the Muslims worldwide.

However, Allah as a term, as a personage (creator of the universe), and as a Christian word for the creator of the universe and maker of the human race was not created by the early Christian Arabs either; they took it from the Aramaic word "Alaahaa", and from the Phoenician word "El" ("Baal-El").

And so did the Hebrews and so many other civilizations and religions throughout the centuries.

The Jewish-Hebrew-Judaic-Israelite Jehovah-Yahweh (Yahweh-Elohim) was the Phoenician god "El", "El-Baal", "Baal Hadad", also called Yaw, Yehaw, and Yehi in Phoenician

The Phoenician "El" became "Eli" in Aramaic. And Jesus on the cross before relinquishing his last breath, called his heavenly father "Eli".

On the cross, Jesus said: "Eloi, Eloi, lamma sabachthani", or "Eloi, Eloi, lema sabachthani"; Matthew: "Eli, Eli, lama sabachthani", that is to say, "My God, my God, why hast thou forsaken me?" (xxvii, 46).

Mark: "Eloi, Eloi, lama sabachthani", which is being interpreted, "My God, my God, why hast thou forsaken me?" (xv, 34.)

The Hebrews too, used the Phoenician word "EL" as "Eli". The plural of Eli (In Aramaic and Hebrew) is Elohim (My Gods, my Lords, and my Masters).

The Arabs obliged, and the Christian and Muslim Arabs transformed "El" into: Elahi, Ilahi, Allah. All came from the same ancient origin/source: Phoenician, and later, Aramaic.

The Phoenician source:

While it was/is forbidden to pronounce the name of Yahweh in Judaism -and at least out of religious courtesy in modern Jewish tradition- Yahweh was a common name in Phoenicia, and especially in Byblos, Batroun, Sidon, Ras Shamra, Nakoura, Tyre, and Ugarit. And it was written and pronounced in various ways, such as:

a-Yehi,

b-Yehaw,
c-Yehar,
d-Yah,
e-Yehu.
Many Phoenician males were called Yahweh-this, or Yahweh-that. And a few Phoenician kings used Yahweh as part of their first names, such as:
a-Yehaw-milk,
b-Yehar-baal.
For instance, in 1929, a 10th century B.C. inscription on an ancient Phoenician building built by Yehimilk, king of Byblos was found and contained the following:
"May the assembly of the gods of Byblos,
the king of Byblos, and Baal-shamem prolong
the life of Yehi-milk..."

On another fragment of the tablet (Or slab), a passage reads as follows:
"I am Yehaw-milk, the king of Byblos,
the son of Yeh-ar-baal..."
Note: The name Yehi-milk is a very old word composed of two parts:
a-Yehi,
b-Milk, which means king.

From the Phoenician word "Milk", derived the Arabic and Hebrew word Malik/Malak, which also means king.
Not to confuse Malak with Malaak, which means angel in Hebrew, Aramaic and Arabic.
Worth mentioning here that the words/names Yaw, Yeuo and Yaw, which gave birth to the word/name Yahweh were also found on an ancient Phoenician coin in Gaza, made during the Persian Period. The coin had a Phoenician inscription and the image of the Phoenician sea god, then, called Yaw. Numerous historians and archaeologists have argued that the image on the Phoenician coin is indeed the image of the Hebrew Yahweh.

Additional findings revealed that the word Yahweh was used and pronounced differently by the Phoenicians throughout the centuries.

For instance, Yehi-milk was frequently used in the 10th century B.C., while Yehaw-milk was used in the 5th and the 4th centuries B.C., in various regions of Phoenicia and Syria (The Canaanite Land).

Numerous Sumerologists and Assyriologists believe that Yah (Referring to Yahweh) originated from the Assyro-Babylonian word "Ya'u", which was the name of an Assyrian-Babylonian god, and later in history, the words "Ya'u" and "Yah" were written as "Jah" in Mesopotamian epics, poems, and myths. While a greater number of linguists and historians argued that "Ya'u" was an alternative name and a Mesopotamian pronunciation of the Phoenician word "Yau" and/or "Wau".

Jewish Bible (Old Testament) confirmed that Yahweh was called Baal (Name of a Phoenician god) by some Israelites.

From Hosea 2:16: "And in that day, says the Lord, you will call me, 'My Husband,' and no longer will you call me, 'My Ba'al.' For I will remove the names of the Ba'als from her mouth, and they shall be mentioned by name no more."

In conclusion, Yahweh-Elohim, the God of Israel who became the god of the Christians and Muslims, absorbed the names, attributes, descriptions, epithets, and the glorious feats of the gods of Mesopotamia and Canaan, who were his rivals, and became the subject and theme of Israel's prophets hysterical attacks on Phoenicia and Ugarit's gods.

The history of ancient religions of the Middle East and the Near East revealed that Yahweh-Elohim was a colorful amalgam of earlier pagans' gods, centuries before the Jewish Bible was written.

The Israelite Yahweh is de facto, a recast-replica of Yaw, Bel, Baal of the Phoenician-Ugartic myths, and other Anunnaki gods.

Yahweh was already a holy name used in Canaanite literature, centuries before the Mosaic epoch.

Yahweh is a combination of the traits and attributes of Yaw/Yam/Baal of the Phoenician-Ugaritic Myths (1500-1200 B.C.) and Babylon's Anuna, thousands of years before the Hebraic monotheistic religion was established.
The Hebraic scribes and writers of the Old Testament fused the Ugaritic El (Bull-El), Yaw and Baal together into the new image of Yahweh-Elohim of the Jewish Bible.

The Phoenician words "Yehaw", "Yehi", "Yaw", and "Yeuo" are the origin of the Hebrew words "Yah", "Yahu", and "Yahweh".
The Phoenician name Yehaw-milk, which was also used as Yehi, Yehaw, and Yehar which meant "Yehaw is king", as well as the name of the Phoenician/Canaanite sea-god Yaw or Yeuo gave birth to the Hebrew words Yah, Yahweh and Yahu.

The image of Yaw/Yeuo which was found on a ancient coin from Gaza, made during the Persian period of Greek artifact and craftsmanship, was in fact, the first historical image of the Hebrew God, Yahweh; a god, the Phoenicians worshipped under the name of Yehi-milk (10th century B.C.) and Yehaw-milk (5th/4th century B.C.)
As soon as the Israelites destroyed the Canaanites (Syrians and Phoenicians), they ascribed all the mighty and supernatural attributes, powers, deeds and glory of the Canaanite and Mesopotamian gods to their own and newly created "GOD" Yahweh.
And Yahweh became the one and only true god, not Baal, El, or Bel. And afterward, Christianity and Islam used the same scenario.
To the Christians, Jesus became God. And to the Muslims, Allah became the one and only god, not Jesus, Yaw, Yahweh, Baal or Bel.
The absolute truth is that the newly created Hebrew god "Yahweh" is de facto, an amalgam of the Mesopotamian, Egyptian, Hittite, and Canaanite (Syrian and Phoenician) gods and goddesses.
Linguists, theologians and historians of religions, easily recognized the new divine persona and attributes given to God

199

Yahweh by the Hebrews, simply by comparing the new Hebrew's attributions to their god, with the old epithets and attributes of gods Baal Saphon (Baal Hadad), El, Seth, Sopdu, Shamash, Tammuz, Anu, Enki, and Enlil. If you compare the epithets and attributes of the Anunnaki god Marduck with those of Yahweh and Allah, you will find out that they are almost identical.

Marduck had 50 to 90 titles. Allah has "99 Asma' Al Lah Al-Housna", which means the 99 noble names of Allah, and Yahweh is no exception.

Israelites bore the name of the Phoenician god Baal:

It is a fact that a considerable number of the early Israelites bore the name of God Baal, as did and still do, people from neighboring countries, and even in Latin America, through out the centuries.

Millions of Muslims have as a first name "Mohammad", which is the name of the Prophet Mohammad.

In Latin America, the tradition continues to the present day; there are hundreds of thousands of men who are called Jesus. So, it is not unconceivable that some Israelites bore the name of Phoenician deities such as Baal.

Sons of Saul, the first king of Israel were called Baal. And as told by Hosea, Yahweh was also called Baal. But the trend of naming Israelites Baal ceased when Israel waged a war against the Ugaritic and Phoenicians when the Hebrew prophets and scribes began to feel the direct threat of the Phoenician religion to their Judaism and Hebraic religion, between 1200 and 587 B.C.

Appearances of the word Yahweh outside and before the Bible was written (To name a few):

The word Yahweh and its divine elements were found:

1-In inscriptions on Ramesses III's temple in Medinet Habu, which contained the words Yah-wa and Yi-ha, which scholars and linguists have associated these 2 Syrian words with the Hebrew word Yah-weh, circa 1400 B.C.

2-On the list of Rameses II, which was discovered in an ancient Nubian temple in Amara (Amarah). Number of listing: 93-98.

200

3-In the Canaanite inscription "Yah of Gat" on an ewer from the late Bronze Age, which was found in the ruins of a temple at Lachish.

4-On the "Stele of Mesh'a", Anet 320 (9th century).

5-An archaeological excavation which revealed the names of Aramean princes from the 8th B.C., which contained the element Yau, and which was occasionally pronounced Yah.

6-In an ostracon from Kuntillet Ajrud 246, from the 8th century.

7-In the Egyptian list of names of places, which was discovered in Amon temple of Amenhotep III, located in Soleb in Nubia.

8-In the Adad and Lachish letters, Anet, 569, 322, from the 6th century.

9-In the Murashu archives from the reign of Artaxerxes and Darius, discovered at Nippur, and which contained the word Ja-a-ma (Jawa), which is associated with the divine element of Yahweh.

10-In an ancient Egyptian clay tablet referring to Ahi-Jami, the mayor of Ta'anach in Canaan. Ahi-Jami was also pronounced and written as Ahi-ja and Ahi-Yah; two names closely related to the divine status of Yahweh, at the time it was referred to and written as Ja-mi (Yah-mi).

Said tablet can be found in the archives of the Museum of Cairo.

11-In an archeological find referring to Sa-rar (Also known as Seir in Edom) which historians and archaeologists have associated Yahweh with Seir and Paran.

12-In the lists of Egyptian names which contained the name and location of an ancient site in Syria, called Yah-wa, Number's reference 97.

13-Three Amorite tablets displayed at the British Museum in 1908, which contained "Yaum-ilu", "Ya'we-ilu", and "Yawe-ilu", referring to the three ancient forms of the primordial name of Yahweh as 'Jahweh is God".

Worth noting here that "Yah", corresponds to the Biblical "Jah" of Psalm 114:35. There is no doubt that the first component of "Ya'wa-ilu" is the name of Yahweh.

14-In the list of names at Mari, from the second millennium B.C., and Yahweh appeared as an Amorite name under Yahwi.

15-In Assyrian records: In the annals of Tiglathpileser III which included the name of Azri-Yau, who was a Syrian king.

We should keep in mind that Yahweh was worshiped in Syria and Phoenicia and not just in Israel.

And it was customary for Canaanite kings to have Yahwehistic names, especially in the first millennium B.C. Yahwehistic names also appeared during the reign of Sargon II.

In fact, numerous Assyrian texts and records included those names and their elements. One of those names mentioned in the Assyrian records was Yau-bidi, a ruler of Hamath.

16-In the Mari archives from the second millennium B.C. (circa 18th century B.C.) which contained names of Amorites known to be Yahweh's names, such as: Yawiya, Yawidim, Yawium, Yawiila, Yawid, Yausib, and Yawi.

Worth mentioning here, the derivation and relation of Yahweh, Yausib, Yaahwi and Yaahwi, and their causative verbal forms. Yaah-wi derived from the Ugaritic and Phoenician word "hwy", which also appeared as "hyw" in Ethiopian, and as "hyy" in Arabic, Aramaic and Hebrew, and meant "be, to be, to become, and to give life."

However, if could also mean "to appear, to be present, and to manifest" taken into consideration the definition and meaning of the word "yahwi" (yaahwi) in Amorite. The two similar sentences in Amorite and archaic Phoenician-Proto Ugaritic "Yaahwi ilum" and "Yahwi ilu" mean the god who manifests himself. The word "ilu" and related elements were concurrently used as "el", "il", "eli", "Ilum" (Akkadian), in Phoenician, Ugaritic, Hebrew and even Arabic, since the Arabic words "Ilahi" (My god), "Ilah" (God) and "Alaah" were used in ancient and modern Arabic.

Yawi (Ya-wi) is obviously a variant of "Yaah-wi (Ya-ah-wi). Grosso modo, it is epistemologically based upon "hwy", which is associated with the Akkadian "ewu", the Aramaic "hwh" and "hwy".

17-In the letter sent by Iawa-ila "Iawi-Ilâ", the Syrian king of Talhayum to Zimri-lim king of Mari (circa1782-1759 B.C.)

Note: The element "iawi" of the Amorite names and the Hebrew god's name originated from the same root, and was considered a divine name in both Hebrew and Amorite languages.

The Amorite names "Iawi-Ila", "Iawi Abdu", "Iahwi-Nasi", and "Iwahi-Sibu" also appeared in the "Mari Archives". God Nasi is a form of the word "Malik" (King). The word or term "Nasi" in archaic Hebrew is closely associated with "Elohim" (God/Gods).

Numerous Orientalists, Assyriologists and Sumerologists have suggested that Yahweh should be rendered ya'wa.

18-On the 10th century B.C. inscription on an ancient Phoenician building built by Yehimilk (Yehi-milk), king of Byblos, which was discovered in 1929.

19-In late old Babylonian Texts (circa 1800-1600 B.C.) where several Amorite personal names were mentioned with a "yawi" element, such as Yawium, the King of Kish (Modern day Tall al-Uhaymir), a contemporary of Abraham who lived nearby.

Numerous scholars, Assyriologists and linguists agreed that the form "yawi" of Mari Archives (circa 1800-1700 B.C) and "Yawium" of Kish (circa 1800-1600 B.C.) among other texts from Ur and Babylon which clearly mentioned all the elements and epistemological derivations of Yah-weh, retrace the origin of the Hebrew word/name Yahweh and Yahwehism.

And since Abraham who lived around 1800-1600 B.C. in that part of the world, it is logical to conclude that he learned about a god called Yahweh, and about "Yawi" and consequently borrowed the names and added his Biblical twist upon.

The origins of Yahwehism:

The origins of Yahwehism are not found in the Sinai Desert-Negeb as falsely claimed by the scribes of the Old Testament. It is proven by archaeology, forensic anthropology, and philology that Yahwehism originated in, and from the Phoenician cities of Ugarit and Mari in Syria, and Ur of the Chaldees/Sumer.

The Israelites/Hebrews admitted that their ancestors were Arameans/Syrians.

Deuteronomy 26:5 "And thou shalt speak and say before the Lord thy God: 'A Syrian ready to perish was my father; and he went down into Egypt and sojourned there with a few, and became there a nation, great, mighty, and populous."

Other translation: Deuteronomy 26:5 (CEB "Common English Bible"): "Then you should solemnly state before the Lord your God: My father was a starving Aramean.
He went down to Egypt, living as an immigrant there with few family members, but that is where he became a great nation, mighty and numerous."

In the Pentateuch, the Hebrew scribes fused two separate and totally different stories and historical origins of two periods:
a-The Bronze Age Canaanite.
b-The Iron Age Aramean.
In 560 B.C., the Hebrew scribes who wrote the story of the Exodus (2 Kings 25:27) were totally ignorant of the fact that their "Newly named and discovered" Yahweh, existed already under similar or quasi-similar names in much older scriptures, texts and stories from the Bronze Age, and Yahweh's attributes were taken from the attributes and epithets of the gods of Ugarit, Mari, Sumer, Egypt and other regions of Canaan, such as Enki of Mesopotamia, Baal-Zephon of the Hyksos, Baal-Hadad, and Bel of Ugarit, Tyre, Sidon and Byblos, and Seth of Egypt.
In deity's imagery:
Phoenicia was the original source for the Hebrew Yahweh's imagery in the Bible and the "Cherubim Throne".
The Phoenician gods seated on the winged sphinx thrones of Byblos (Identical to the Anunnaki-Sumerian thrones) were the prototypes of Yahweh's Cherubim throne in the Temple of Jerusalem.
The Hebrews transmuted the sphinx into angels (Cherubim). As a matter of fact, the early Hebrew Cherubim were depicted as humans with the heads of winged sphinxes.
According to 1 Sam 4:4, Yahweh, the God of Israel was "He who sitteth (on) the cherubim."
In addition, many Phoenician kings (Messengers of the Gods) were depicted as divine monarchs seated on a large stone or marble throne (Circa 1200-800 B.C.) supported on each side by cherubim, and found in Megiddo, Byblos (Modern day Jbeil), Hamath and Tyre (Modern day Sour). The most famous throne belonged to King Hiram of Phoenicia seated on a cherub throne.

Yahweh also sat on a cherub throne.

Yahweh-Elohim and the Phoenician-Ugaritic Bull-Gods and the golden calves: Short after the alleged apparition of Yahweh-Elohim to Moses at Mt. Sinai as a thundercloud, a Hebraic golden calf was fashioned in a Phoenician style.
Apparently, there is a connection between the Phoenician "Calf" and the Israelites' reason for fashioning their own golden calf.
At that time in history, the Hebrew god was depicted as "Bull-Calf" in the image of the Phoenician, Ugaritic and Hyksos gods, Bull-El, and Baal-Hadad of the Bronze Age. The "Bull" image or at least the "Bull" symbol played a paramount role in the early Hebrew Scriptures and beliefs.
This, became evident and unquestionable when the Hebrews used the Hyksos-Ugaritic Bull (Baal-Hadad) as symbol for their escape from Egypt.

The thundercloud imagery:
The sons of the Phoenician god Bull-El were born as bull-calves according to the Phoenician mythology. And one of his sons, the great god Baal-Hadad (Also known as Adad) is quite often depicted as a huge bull with sparkling lightning bolts surrounded by thunderclouds called the calves of Adad.
The thunderclouds, the heavy cloud, the thick darkness and the loud voice were the main characteristics of the Phoenician Bull-Gods. The Hebraic God Yahweh appeared quite often in the form of a thundercloud. And as described in the Old Testament (The Jewish Bible), at Mount Sinai, Yahweh appeared to Moses as a "Thundercloud". It is obvious that the Biblical thundercloud, and the voice of Yahweh as thunder were borrowed from a Phoenician mythical imagery.
According to the Epic of Gilgamesh, Baal-Hadad is a god who lives in a thundercloud.
According to Deuteronomy 4:11 and 5:22, Yahweh too lives in a thundercloud. In addition, the voice of the Phoenician Bull-Gods was "Thunder". And so is the voice of the Hebraic god Yahweh: Thunder! This is not a coincidence, but rather a "copiage" of the much older Phoenician-Ugaritic-Mesopotamian myths.

205

Deuteronomy 4:11: "And you came near and stood at the foot of the mountain, while the mountain burned with fire to the heart of heaven, wrapped in darkness, cloud and gloom."
Deuteronomy 5:22,23: "These words the Lord spoke to all your assembly at the mountain out of the midst of the fire, the cloud, and the thick darkness with a loud voice..."
From the Epic of Gilgamesh, "There rises from the foundation of the heavens a black cloud. Adad thunders in the midst of it..."

Alad "Alada": Sumerian/Anunnaki. Noun.
In Sumerian, Alad means two things:
a-A guardian angel;
b-A spirit watching over and protecting a person.
It is derived from the Anunnaki's word Alada, which means two things:
a-Internal strength created by life energy;
b-A protective guide.
Worth mentioning here, that while the majority of the guardian angels "Alad" in Assyrian, Chaldean, Sumerian, Akkadian, Babylonian and Mesopotamian culture and mythologies were males, the "Alada", also called "Alaada-Shalim" were females. This is quite obvious, since the Anunnaki's society is matriarchal in nature, and the Anunnaki family's affairs are under the direct control of the wife/mother.

Aldebaran:
1. Definition: Also called Ashtari, and Alpha Tauri, the planet of the Anunnaki. It is the brightest star in the Hyades; a giant red star in the constellation of Taurus; one of the 15 brightest stars with a visual magnitude of 0.85. Its diameter is 44 times that of the Sun. It is accompanied by a very faint (13th magnitude) red companion star. Aldebaran lies 65 light-years from Earth. The star was once thought to be a member of the Hyades cluster, but in fact Aldebaran is 85 light-years closer to Earth. Aldebaran was nicknamed "The Follower" because it rises after the Pleiades cluster of stars. A NASA trusted scientist reported that in 1972, NASA sent a message to the people of Aldebaran, and another one via Pioneer 10.

2. Aldebaran (Ashtari) in ancient religions, mythology, astrology and esoteric studies:

a-The Hindu masters called it Rohoni.

b-The Phoenicians referred to it as the Eye of the Universe.

c-To the ancient Persians, Aldebaran (Ashtari) was one of the four royal stars, and considered to be the star of wisdom and enlightenment.

d-Aldebaran inaugurated the beginning of the Babylonian year, some 5,100 years ago.

e-In the "Book of Chaldea", Aldebaran was mentioned as the "guiding light -on the physical passage- toward the realms of the gods (Extraterrestrials).

f-The ancient Habiru (Early Hebrews) called it the Eye of Il "El" (God).

g-Eastern ascetics and numerous Buddhist monks called it the Star of the Buddha.

h-The Rouhaniyiin called it the realm of the Mounawiriin (The Enlightened Ones).

i-The early Akkadians called it the passage to heaven.

j-Ashtari was known to the Arabs as Aldebaran.

The verb "Adbara" in Arabic means: He left, he moved away, he traveled, he walked away. And the correct meaning of the word Aldebaran is NOT "who he follows, or the follower" as tragically interpreted by Encyclopedia Britannica! And I am puzzled and astonished by Britannica's wrong definition of Aldebaran!!

Al Debaran or AlDaber means, "he who moved away, who left, who traveled", and the Arabic verb is "Adbara". Any person who speaks Arabic knows what "Adbara" means. The Arab nomads and early tribes in the Middle East, including the Persian Gulf and the Arab Peninsula have used the verbs "Idbir" and "Adbar" in their spoken dialect, and written language.

Aldebaran was mentioned in two important books:

- 1-The Anunnaki Ulema "Book of Ramadosh",
- 2-The Arabic book "Ilmu Al Donia" (Science or Knowledge of the world".

So, Aldebaran is Ash.Ta.Ri, the constellation of the Anunnaki, and the home of the extraterrestrials beings of lights Maria told us about. But keep in mind, that the Aldebaran's aliens are not the Anunnaki, but an offspring of the Anunnaki, sharing the same galactic genes.

And yes, both descended on Phoenicia, Mesopotamia and the Anatolian plateau of Asia Minor (Turkey and Armenia) 450,000-460,000 B.C. The Aldebarans' extraterrestrials who were part of the Anunnaki's expedition to Earth, took part in establishing civilizations in the Near East, Middle East and Asia Minor.

Some of their colonies were:

- Eridu
- Uruk
- Nippur
- Nineveh
- Lagash
- Ur
- Umma
- Assur
- Ebla
- Saydoon (Sidon, Saida)
- Tyrakh (Tyre, Sour)
- Kadmosh
- Adonakh
- Ilayshim
- Markadash (Byblos to the Greeks, and Jbail to the Arabs)
- Baalbeck, where we find the legendary "Hajarat Al Houblah"
- Ugarit

These cities and their civilizations are mentioned in the ancient scriptures, slabs, and clay tablets of the Middle East, Near East, the Phoenician Cosmogony, the Sumero-Akkadian epics written in cuneiform, and the Bible.

Maria Orsic was right when she said that the Aldebaran's people created civilizations in Mesopotamia (Sumeria, Babylon, Akkad, so on), and they came from Aldebaran (Ash.Ta.Ri, Alpha Tauri).
Some authors and well-known hosts of TV shows on aliens have claimed that Nibiru is the planet of the Anunnaki and the ancient alien gods, because the Sumerian tablets said so!
If this is the case, then Maria Orsic's claims are wrong! No! Maria was right, and they are wrong because the Sumerian epics never mentioned Nibiru as the home-planet of the Anunnaki; those people need -first- to learn Akkadian and Sumerian before they interpret epics written in languages they can't read.

The Anunnaki-Ulema have revealed to us that some planets in our galaxy, as well as in Ashtari constellation are positioned on a 33.33 degree line which serves as "Ba'ab" (Gateway) to other galaxies and dimensions. This 33.33 degree line was mentioned by Maria Orsic.
Ashtari constellation has millions upon millions of stars and planets, and many of them are a physical stargate, the Anunnaki Ulema call "an opening on" multiple universes and dimensions, including the astronomical bodies of the physical galaxies, and celestial ones that escape time and space, even before time was created, and since time existed as another dimension outside the landscape of the physical universe; this is incomprehensible to the human mind.

3. Maria Orsic description of Aldebaran (Ashtari):
Maria Orsic' description of Aldebaran is identical to the description of Ash.Ta.Ri, given by Anunnaki Sinhar Ambar Anati to American scientists and United States government officials and which we have on record.
It is also similar to the description of other inhabitable planets in the Aldebaran constellation and other constellations given by the female alien Riyah to American generals, linguists and scientists in 1947.
The three extraterrestrials' descriptions can be compared in the "1947-1948 Aliens Transcripts", "Mouzakarat Sinhar Marduk", "Book of Ramadosh", and "Kitabu Ilmu Al Donia".

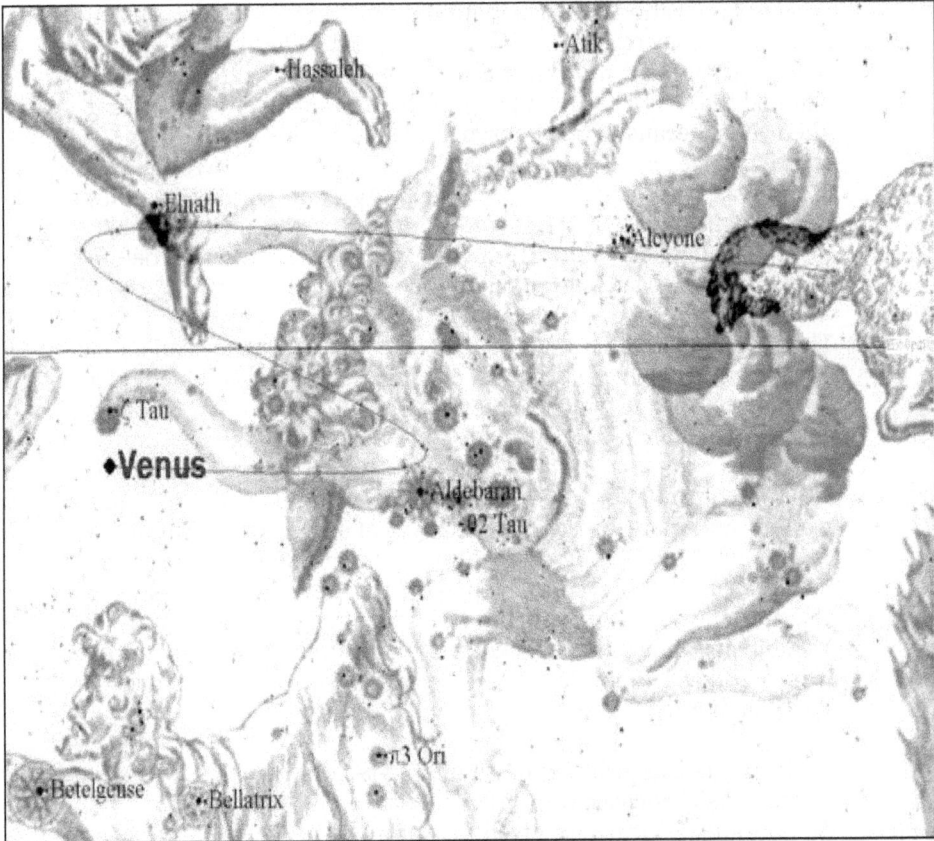

Astrological location of Aldebaran.

Aldebaran, from the files of NASA.

Albebaran
Red Giant

Aldebaran

Aldebaran is accompanied by Aldebaran B, (Alpha Tauri B, the home of the extraterrestrials who contacted Maria) a planet that contains water, lots of water, and it supports life.

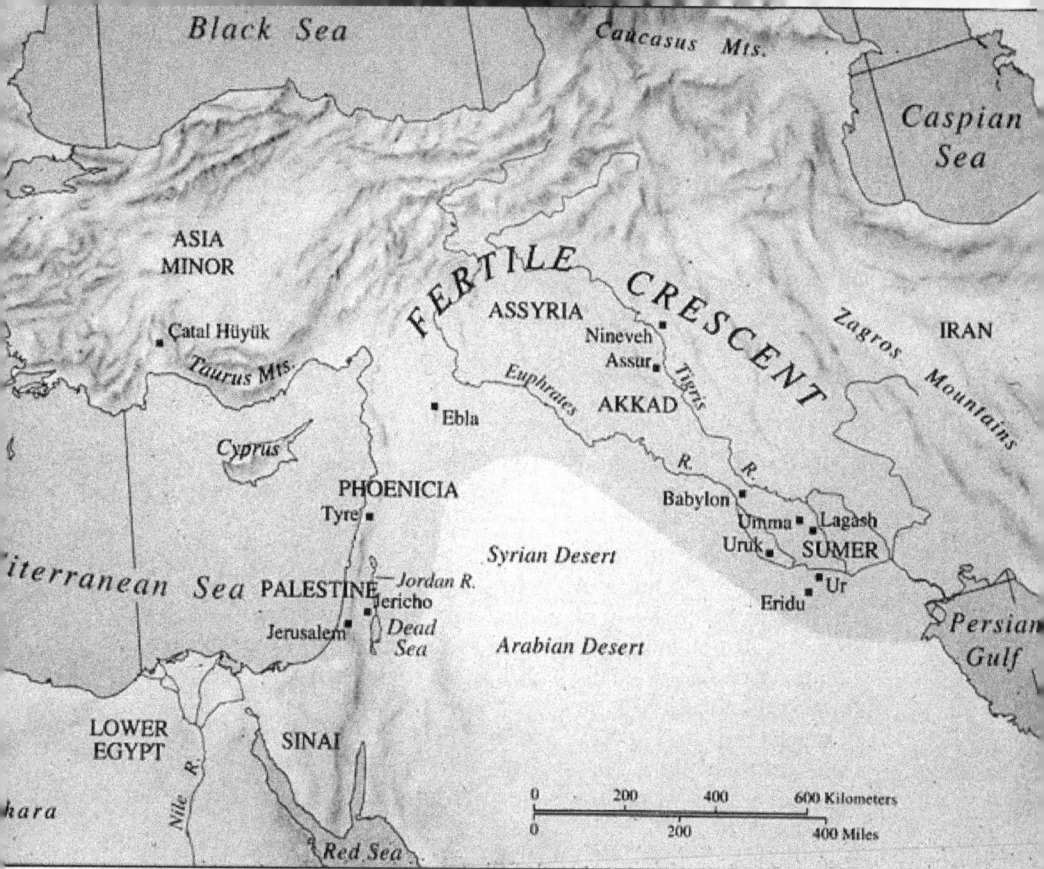

Map of Sumer, showing the location of the Anunnaki cities:
Babylon, Lagash, Uruk, Ur and Eridu.

Days' calendar and moons around the inhabitable planets in
Aldebaran: A day consists of forty-eight hours.

The sun rises around four o'clock in the morning, and the sunrise
takes about two hours and twenty five minutes; the colors in the
sky at that time are spectacular.

The sun shines for eighteen hours in the summer and for twelve
hours in the winter; there are only two seasons on their planets.

The sun then takes two hours for sunsets. Ash.Ta.Ri (The planet
of the Anunnaki) has four moons. All moons rise harmoniously
one after the other, and line up in four different directions. The
home-planet of the Aldebaran's extraterrestrials has two moons
and two planets rotating around it. The moons of each planet
stay for about ten hours. And when they fade away, they follow
the same pattern, one after the other in the same synchronized
manner.

Atmosphere and energy:
a-No pollution.
b-No smokes from factories.
c-No oil fuels.
d-Pure electromagnetic energy is used exclusively.
The term "electromagnetic" is not totally correct. But this is as close as we get to understand its properties.
Their energy consists of a blend of spatial neuro-plasma and subatomic molecules. And even these wordings are not correct because on planet earth, blending or fusing these elements and substances together contradict mainstream science.
Waters, lands and lakes: There are plenty of canals, and so much water on their planet; about fifty/fifty to the land, the ratio is, but they have some wonderful lakes underground which are as blue as a sapphire.

Adjacent planets and other extraterrestrials:
Inhabitants of adjacent planets vary sharply from one civilization to another, but all are highly advanced, and have one thing in common, which is very characteristic of their climate: An anti-pollution shield that protects their atmosphere.
On Earth, it is the Ozone.
In the Aldebaran's solar system, there are two small planets that support life, and are inhabited by people who resemble us. They have evolved very slowly, and are considered by other galactic civilizations to be inferior, "even savages", because they eat meat and fight.
At the far edge of their solar system there are four planets which are totally different from their habitat, because none has an atmosphere. They are cold, and sterile.
And their inhabitants don't look like us physically; in fact their appearance will scare the hell out of us, because some look like machines, while others like huge insects and reptilians.
Other civilizations are aware of their existence, but they avoid them because they are hostile and very aggressive; they belong to the forces of darkness. Maria Orsic like Sinhar Anati talked about the Lyran system which consisted of 9 planets and 13 moons. The Lyrans, Aldebarans and Anunnaki are on very good terms.

The Aldebaran's extraterrestrials are the offspring of a higher race (The Anunnaki) which visited Earth hundreds of thousands of years ago, and created the earliest civilizations on Earth. Some lived on Earth for thousands of years but eventually returned back to Aldebaran. Others got stuck on Earth and could not make it home. Consequently they lost their extraterrestrial genes, and began to look like humans, gradually.

Yet, they were very advanced and created wonders on Earth.

Some were killed by the Great Deluge, and those who survived, returned after a while to:

- Mount Hermon (Jabal Haramoun)
- Baalbeck
- Lake Van
- Urartu
- Dilmun (Ancient Bahrain)
- Hadramout (Yemen)
- Anatolia
- Mesopotamia
- Himalaya mountains
- Tibet
- Scandinavia
- And to scattered islands in the Mediterranean.

All are considered to be Aryans, even though the Anunnaki have black eyes and black hair, with the exception of the higher cast of the Anunnaki which has light black hair and blue eyes.

Effects on humans upon arrival to Aldebaran-Ashtari:

Orsic's dream was to visit the extraterrestrials of Aldebaran. And she asked them lots of questions about their habitats, lifestyle and whether she could live there with her Ladies of Vril. Here is a synopsis of what we already know about the physiological, psychological and emotional effects on humans upon arrival to Aldebaran-Ashtari.

Upon Arrival:

When a human being arrives to Ashtari-Aldebaran for the first time, he or she experiences new physiological, emotional and psychological effects, as well as psychosomatic reactions.

215

The extraterrestrials told Maria (Similar account by Anunnaki Sinhar Anati) that the very first thing she will see when she steps out of the spaceship could be described as a quantum jump into a world which looks like a sand storm on a completely gray planet.

At the very beginning, said the extraterrestrials to Maria, you will feel horrible and becomes dizzy. It is the atmosphere of our planet that causes this. You need three days to adjust.

The following is an excerpt from Anunnaki Sinhar Anati which perfectly illustrates the situation, Maria will be in, the moment she enters the world of her extraterrestrial friends:

The first thing the Aldebaran-Anunnaki extraterrestrials will do, is to take you to a bright room. A gentle person will show you the way to a bedroom.

This person exchanges a few words with you and directs you to a very comfortable bed. And you will appreciate that, because by then you will be extremely tired, and you will sleep instantly. The next day you will wake up, and the treatment of your sight begins. A person dressed in lilac will show you to a room with a basin filled with aquamarine-tinted fluid.

This person will ask you to go in, relax, and think only about colors, nothing else, preferably about one specific color, and this person would come back in an hour or so. The bathtub makes you feel good. The bathtub is perfumed with some floral scent you will not recognize, but you will like a lot.

For a while nothing happens, but after a few minutes, all of a sudden a stream of lavender light fills the basin and then lifts up and surrounds you like a beautiful web. At the same moment, and to your surprise, if on earth you had any muscular or joint pain, it will totally disappear. All these are part of adjusting your vision; they (Extraterrestrials) must cure all the weaknesses of the human body, genes, and all the possible diseases and sicknesses that you might have in the future, in order to readjust your sight.

On the second day, the same person (An extraterrestrial) leads you through a connecting corridor to a surgical room in another building. You will be introduced to a nurse, or a physician, who will ask you to lie down on a table. A machine comes from the ceiling, shining a laser-like beam.

The machine scans your brain, and the nurse will ask you to look at the screen on your right side to see how the cells in your brain would create new visual faculties. This is absolutely amazing.

You could actually see how your brain works. The nurse explains to you that many cells, millions of particles of your brains, were never used by you and now many of them would become yours to use. After a short time, the nurse puts a soft but firm bandage around your eyes and a metallic band or a belt around your forehead.

The band or the belt readjusts the level of energy and reactivates part of your brain's cells. The band or the belt also develops a telepathic power in due time.

At a later day, you will be able to communicate telepathically with us. Pictures start to flow into your head and you don't know where they come from. Some are the faces of other beings you have never met in your life. It is a very strange feeling. You see faces and other things, but you do not hear sounds or voices. And everything happens calmly without any mental or physical effort. When the treatment is over, your vision becomes perfect.

And soon, you could go out and see the planet for the first time. Outside, the air is pure, and the sky is full of rainbows of colors. You have never seen such colors in your entire life, because these colors do not exist on earth. Some of the colors of the sky blend with the colors of the landscape, giving you the feeling that the ground is united with the sky.

Then, you realize that something very strange is happening to you; your vision is no longer limited to straight lines. Now, you can see, magically, to the left and to the right, like a surrounding vision. And you start to see more and more things; absolutely stunning buildings glimmered under the brilliant sky, trees, bushes, and flowers everywhere and beautifully dressed, smiling people walking in the streets. How different from what you saw first, a gray planet with swirling sand in its atmosphere!

Immediate impression and reactions:

Those who landed on the Aldebaran-Ashtari constellation for the first time experienced something very unique; an optical problem, a psycho-somatic vision/sight anomaly, more precisely, the inability of seeing.

217

Temporarily they become totally blind. This phenomenon and how to regain sight was described by Sinhar Ambar Anati.

Note: Anati is describing what happened to her upon her arrival to Ashtari and she is talking to her Anunnaki relatives.
In her own words:
"Why can't I see anything outside?
It's the atmosphere. There is no pollution, no smoke, no oil fuels, since pure electromagnetic energy is all the Anunnaki use. It is so bright, so clear, that it creates a strange effect on the human retina, which is accustomed to different conditions...
When I woke up, my treatment began. Miriam (An Anunnaki female) took me to a little room where she showed me a basin filled with aquamarine-tinted fluid.
She asked me to go in, relax, and think only about colors, nothing else, preferably about one specific color. She would come back in an hour or so, she said, and the water will stay warm as long as I was in.
I climbed into the bath which felt wonderful and was fragrant with some floral scent I did not recognize. I closed my eyes and thought about the color lavender, beautiful, gentle soft kind of lavender.
For a while nothing happened, but after a few minutes, all of a sudden a stream of lavender light filled the basin and then lifted and surrounded me like a beautiful web. To my surprise, at the same moment, a joint pain I developed on earth disappeared. It was in my ankle, which I have hurt a year ago while running, and it did not heel properly, giving me occasional pain.
I twisted it when I left the spaceship and stumbled, and it hurt when I woke up from my nap. Now it was perfectly well. Later they explained that as they adjust the vision, they must cure all the weaknesses of the human body, my genes, and all the possible disease and sicknesses that I might have in the future. Even at my young age I could feel the difference between the human condition and perfect health. On the second day, Miriam led me through a connecting corridor to a surgical room in another building.

They have these corridors, connecting houses and buildings to each other, and they never lock any doors.

Such a trusting, simple lifestyle, such a pleasure.

She introduced me to a nurse, or physician, who asked me to lie down on a table.

I did, and a machine came from the ceiling, shining a laser-like beam. Apparently, they scanned my brain, and the nurse told me to look at the screen on my right side and see how the cells in my brain would create new visual faculties.

This was utterly amazing. I could actually see how the human brain worked! The nurse explained that many cells, millions of particles of the brains, are never used by humans, and now many of them would become mine to use. After a short time, the nurse put a bandage around my eyes and a metallic band around my forehead.

This was needed for readjusting the energy and reactivating part of the cells. They told me that this will not only adjust my vision, but will develop a telepathic power in due time.

Indeed, to my great delight and astonishment, at a later day I was able to communicate telepathically with the Anunnaki, at will. When the treatment was completed, my vision was perfect, and Miriam told me that I could go out and see their world for the first time."

4. Maria Orsic explains the world of extraterrestrials:

Ethics and family: Aldebaran and Ashtari extraterrestrials live in a world our human logic and mind can't understand. Although they (The extraterrestrials) do not practice any religion, their sense and understanding of ethics, justice, good and evil deeds, and merits are well developed.

They see the universe, the development of the mind and a person's character quite differently from the way we do.

They take into a great consideration the consequences of an act, even a miniscule thought. They don't have courts of law, trials, tribunals, prosecutors, judges, lawyers and corporal punishment, but they have established rules that govern behavior, merits, deeds, and social justice.

"Their families, parents, children, relatives, and members of their communities are guided by social ethics and a moral law, far superior to our laws and religions...they have families like us...they feel like us...they work together in a perfect harmony, using a collective awareness shared by all..." said Maria.
(Note: This is exactly what Sinhar Anati said, and which I have published in one of my books on the Anunnaki.)

Worth mentioning here what Anunnaki Ulema Najani said on the subject: "The Anunnaki have families, fathers, mothers, and children too, and they follow familial hierarchy, and family morality rules as we do here on Earth..."
Anunnaki Ulema Albard said, "Unlike other extraterrestrial races and species that are not built around family structure and parental bonds, the Anunnaki live within their own families perimeter, and show feelings and emotional reactions as we do..." He added, "The head of a living unit or a family is the father. However, the family is always placed under the direct guidance of a mother. Anunnaki society is matriarchal."

Extraterrestrial Karma, body's cells and mind:
The word "Karma" does not exist in their vocabulary, for they don't have the concept of reincarnation. Even though, physical death does not exist in their world, as we understand death on earth, all reach a point when and where the last cell of energy in their bodies ceases to function, thus resulting in the deterioration of their cells.
"After the deterioration of their cells...after they have lived for hundreds of thousands of years, their physical body that they were currently using fades away, but their mind recreates itself as a new copy of the physical body, because, each one of them has a multitude of copies of their body.
They can activate and reactivate the last fully functional and healthy cell of the Vril (In this context, by Vril, Maria meant the quasi-eternal cosmic energy of the self, including the universe), and reproduce it in a large quantity, and activate each newly created cell separately, thus recreating multiple copies of themselves, and restore them in a reversed eternal time storage.

On Aldebaran, I will never age, and my mind will grow healthier and wiser..." said Maria.

Aldebaran's Akashic library:
Learning from the Adelbaran's Extraterrestrials and Anunnaki:
"I am not afraid to go to Aldebaran, Jamara (Name of a planet rotating in their constellation) and Nimra (Another planet), for they (Extraterrestrials) told me that everything is going to be fine. Heike was concerned because we don't know their language and their habits. But they told me once we are there, they will reconstruct our minds and bodies, and we will never suffer again or get sick. Their world is peaceful and beautiful. They will teach me many new things and I will learn about the greatest secrets in the universe...I will have access to their universal libraries which contains the Akashic records of the universe.

I found Maria's statements mind-bending, because they mirror what exactly the Enlightened Anunnaki Ulema told us centuries ago. The Honorable Masters explained to us that the Anunnaki and Aldebaran Akashic Library is not a library in the traditional sense, because it contains no physical books on shelves.

Each one of them (Extraterrestrials) has access to the global Akashic Records through the Akashic libraries, which are located in every community.

One enters through a huge door that is never closed, day and night. It opens into a huge hall, seven hundred to one thousand meters in length, by five hundred meters in width.

The hall is empty of any furniture, and is lit by windows that are placed very high, near the ceiling. The windows were designed in such a way that the shafts of light that enter through them are very sharply delineated and look like solid beams of light. At night, the same effect is achieved by enormous spot lights placed near the windows.

The effect is incredibly effective. Extremely large billboards hang on each wall. On the floor in front of each billboard are hundreds of pads. When visitors enter the library, they approach the billboard, stand each on a pad, and think about their destination within the building.

The pad has the capacity to read minds, and as soon as it does so, it begins to move, and it slides right through the billboard, which is not really solid but is made of a form of energy, carrying the visitor with it.

Behind the billboard is the main hall of the Akashic Library, called Mad-Khal. The visitors find themselves in the presence of an immense screen, composed of a material not found on Earth. The screen is hard to describe; it can be compared to a grid, with a multitude of matrices and vortices of data.

The screen is contacted through the Conduit which is located in the brain's cells. The screen can read minds, and it knows right away what information the visitors seek. All what the visitors have to do is stand still in front of the screen, and the data will be displayed in sequences. Of course, the data is not represented by lines, sentences, or paragraphs, but rather by codes.

Each code contains particular information related to an aspect of the subject. For example, if you would like to visit Iraq, 2,000 A.D., Iraq 300 B.C., or Iraq 2,008 B.C., all you have to do is to focus on these dates, and three codes will appear on the screen waiting for your command to open them up.

From this moment on, the Conduit located in your brain and the Screen are communicating in the most direct fashion. The three files (The nearest description of these files would be to call them digital, for the lack of the proper word) will open up. Each one will contain everything that had happened pertaining to that particular date in Iraq.

The Conduit will sort out, classify, and index the particular data for the part of the information the visitor is most interested in.

Then, the information will be stored automatically in the cells of the visitor's brain, increasing the size of the depot of knowledge in the brain.

And because Anunnaki are connected to each other and to their community via the Conduit, the data recently absorbed is sent to other Anunnaki to share it, which is extremely beneficial, since if the data received from the screen is difficult to understand, the Anunnaki community called Jama, or an individual Anunnaki, will send, also automatically, the explanation needed.

This is quite similar to an online technical support on earth, but it is much more efficient since it functions brain-to-brain. Each Anunnaki community have the same kind of center for these mirrors of knowledge which are the Akashic files. The complexity of the centers though, is not the same.

Some of the Akashic Libraries include more perplexing and complicated instruments and tools, which are not readily available to other communities.

These tools include the monitor, which is also called mirror or Miraya in Ana'kh. Each Miraya is under the direct control of a Sinhar (A leader), who serves as custodian and guardian.

It is very important to protect the privacy of every member of the community, because individuals could attempt to tap into the data of the Miraya and have access to the codes of the telepathic communication of others, thus enabling them to read the mind of all the community members, something that is considered highly unethical and absolutely must be avoided.

The screens, by the way, can expand according to the number of codes that the researcher is using. Seven to ten codes are normal. If more codes than that are opened, the screen is fragmented into seven different screens, which are only visible to the mind. An amazing phenomenon occurs at this moment; time and space mingle together and become unified into one great continuum. This enables the researcher to grasp all the information in a fraction of a second.

An added convenient aspect of the Akashic files is the ability of the researcher to access them in the complete privacy of the researcher's home or office, since part the files can be teleported there. But since the private screen is not as complicated as the central one in the Central Library, no multiple screen will open up, only the original one. It is important to understand that the data received is not merely visual. There is much more to it than that.

By the right side of the screen, there are metallic compartments as thin as parchment paper, which serve as a cosmic audio antennae, called Min-Zar. These compartments search for, and bring back, any sound that occurred in history, in any era, and on any planet.

And this is just a minor part of it, because it brings additional sounds from other dimensions, and para-galactic civilizations (Terrestrials and extraterrestrials).

According to the extraterrestrials, every single sound or voice is never lost in the universe. The voice is never lost, because it is energy and it stays in the perimeter of its sphere, call it for now, atmosphere, space, etc. The Anunnaki combined asset of the visual and audio systems provided by the screen, gives anybody the ability to learn languages afforded by the Akashic Library.

This applies to any language – past, present or future, and from any part of the universe.

The researcher can call up a shining globe of light that will swirl on the screen with enormous speed. As it rotates, the effect blends with an audio transmission that comes from the metallic compartments.

In an instant, any language will sink into the brain's cells. On the left side of the screen, there are conic compartments that bring still images of certain important past events. This mini-screen-display informs the researcher that these particular events cannot be altered.

In other words, the Anunnaki cannot go back in the past and change it. The Anunnaki are forbidden to change or alter the events, or even just parts or segments of past events represented on the conic compartment, because these images represent events created by the Anunnaki themselves.

This restriction works as a security device, an essential one. For example, a young Anunnaki cannot visit planet Earth sixty five thousand years ago, enter the genetic lab of the Anunnaki in Sumer or Phoenicia, and change the DNA and the genetic formula originally used by Sinhar Enki, or Sinhar Anu, to create the human race, or the seven prototypes of the human race created by Sinhar Inanna.

Sinhar Inanna herself can go back and change it, but not for use on earth as we know it. She has to transpose it and transport it to another dimension, parallel to the original dimension where the event occurred.

This safeguard means that Sinhar Inanna cannot recreate a new race on our earth by sending us, the current living humans, sixty five thousand years ago back in time, remoulding us, and then bringing us back to the twenty first century as new specie, or a new race.

This would be unethical.

All she could do would be to recreate her own experiment in another dimension.

For instance, Inanna can go back 2,000 years in time and space, reconstruct the DNA of Jesus Christ and create a new Jesus. But the new Jesus will not exist on the map of year 1, or return to Bethlehem to be re-born again. He will be transported as a grown man to another dimension not very much different from the Palestine Jesus knew.

Before the extraterrestrials' screen in the hall of the Akashic Records, more options are available for research, and one of them is a sort of browsing. Inside the screen, there is a slit where the mind of the extraterrestrial can enter as a beam.

This will open the "Ba'abs", or Stargates, to other worlds that the researcher is not even aware of, but appeared randomly as part of the discovery or exploration.

In each slit there is another Akashic file that belongs to other universes, worlds, dimensions, and civilizations, sometimes more advanced than the Aldebaran's people and Anunnaki themselves, where the researcher can either retrieve important information, and/or witness the creation of the future.

It is like going back in the future, because everything that exists in the present, or shall occur in the future, has already occurred in a distant past and needed time to surface and appear before the eyes of the extraterrestrials.

The term Akashic is herewith used because many of us are familiar with what it means and represents, and to a certain extent refers to the contents of historical events and thoughts recorded in "human history."

In the Aldebaran-Anunnaki context, it is the record of cosmic events that occurred in multiple galaxies.

The reason it is called the Akashic/Cosmic Library is because it has equipment that allows the researcher to connect to the Akashic/Cosmic Records; the vast compendium of knowledge encoded in a non-physical plane of existence, in a substance that is called Akasha.

In Ana' kh, it is called Ab.Har, or simply Har.

5. Impregnation operation in Ashtari "Aldebaran":
Known as "An-Ista-Khan-na-reh" in Ana'kh.
The female Anunnaki goes into a very nice hospital-like place. Anunnaki physicians will help her to lie down on a table, much like one of the examination tables in any doctor's office on earth. The attending physicians will be all females, very gentle and extremely skilled. Using a special machine, they will beam a light right through the woman's body; the light will search for her ovaries. Nothing will probe, or hurt, or even annoy the body.

Once the light reaches the ovaries, it will activate one of the eggs, fertilize it, and have it move very smoothly into the uterus. The woman then becomes pregnant, and the fetus will begin to grow. Anunnaki women have the egg removed by the light, placed in a special tube, and grow the baby in a machine. They don't have birth in the same sense humans do, but take the baby home after he or she is ready in the advanced incubator.

This impregnation operation is called "An-Ista-Khan-na-reh". It is composed from the following words:
1-An'h=Creation; first; celestial.
2-Ista or Ishtah=Child; baby; first born.
3-Khan=hospital; operating room.
4-Na=Source; first breath; first nourishment.
5-Reh or Rah=Delivery; reception; relief.

6. Aldebaran's UFO, Jenseitsflugmaschine:
While Maria was still waiting to hear from Professor Schumann, Traute suggested that all of them must meet with people who can help build Jenseitsflugmaschine, the Aldebaran's UFO.

The idea seemed to appeal to some, but not to Sigrun, who, first, distrusted men in general, and second, did not believe that total strangers would be interested in a metaphysical project, at the time, Germany was struggling with economic instability.

At one point, Maria became very reluctant, for she feared that the Aldebaran's technical data could fall into the hands of people who could misuse it.

Following a "Labyrinth Channeling séance", the Ladies of Vril expressed their concern about Hitler and Himmler, and the inevitable; meaning Himmler's domination over their Vril. Maria was absolutely sure that once Heinrich Himmler becomes aware of Jenseitsflugmaschine, he will exploit it as a military weapon, and if the Ladies of Vril will refuse to cooperate with him, he will shoot them on the spot.

Meeting to discuss the Jenseitsflugmaschine:

Maria Orsic and the Ladies of Vril had a total of five meetings with other groups, members of Thule and DHvSS (Die Herren Vom Schwarzen Stein), some of Germany's most distinguished personalities and leading figures in various disciplines, occupations and professions, including physicians, linguists, engineers, theorists, writers, philosophers, financiers, as well as politicians. All the meetings took place in Munich.

They met to discuss the possibility of building a new kind of a super flying machine called Jenseitsflugmaschine, as well as other types of wonder-machines (These machines were discussed much later) which in ufology's jargon are referred to as UFOs.

The first meeting; Tuesday 16, September 1919: Maria met with Professor Winfried Otto Schumann in a cafe on Arcisstraße, not far from the Technical University of Munich.

They had a preliminary discussion about a technical data on how to build a super flying machine, Maria Orsic received from extraterrestrials from Adelbaran. Maria asked him if he was interested in exploring the possibility of building such a machine. Dr. Schumann was very perplexed but did not reject the idea.

He suggested to Maria to gather more data and any other pertinent information for further consideration. It was a brief meeting but promising.

In order to build the Adelbaran's spaceship, many things had to be done:

- 1-All the messages received in an unknown script must be accurately translated.
- 2-The images Maria received telepathically must be interpreted and explained scientifically.
- 3-Joint effort with other psychics/mediums and financiers to get the financing.
- 4-Contact scientists and engineers to decipher and explain the technical data on how to build the spaceship, and especially the Jenseitsflugmaschine's sketches.
- 5-Secure financing from sources not affiliated with the authorities.
- 6-Keep the whole project secret.

Excerpts from Dr. Winfried Otto Schumann's notes on the Jenseitsflugmaschine:

"...I am not sure if Jenseitsflugmaschine could be built. In theory it is possible. I am familiar with the concept of implosion, which has already been discussed by Mr. Schauberger...Dr. Schapeller's experiments were successful, and in essence the technical data as outlined by Maria do not contradict the findings of both Mr. Schauberger and Dr. Schapeller.

I found it fascinating...I am concerned with her request to keep everything secret; I don't think it is possible, especially if the project is to be discussed with other colleagues whose expertise is much needed to develop the project. I need more time to consider the whole situation. But definitely I am very interested. This could be an unprecedented exploration of a new kind of science. May I suggest to your daughter to not mention the extraterrestrials' role in all this?

It could alienate reputable scientists, who could show a serious interest in building Jenseitsflugmaschine..."

Aldebaran's Jenseitsflugmaschine and Stargates line; the 33.33 degree:

Maria Orsic called her super flying machine (UFO to others) a flying machine for another world; a flying machine for the afterlife; a flying machine for another dimension.
Those were revolutionary concepts for her time, or unorthodox "Appellations", to say the least. In her mind, that flying machine could enter and exit a different dimension, part physical and part abstract, simply by positioning the flying machine on a stargates line she called the 33.33 degree line of Earth.

Dr. Winfried Otto Schumann advised her to avoid implicating aliens in this scenario, and particularly the use of scientific words, since she was not a scientist.
The truth is, Maria never used scientific terminology, for herself admitted that she was not familiar with the technical data she has received from the extraterrestrials of Aldebaran.

Comparing Maria's data with Viktor Schauberger and Karl Haushofer data

Professor Schumann began to change his opinion about Maria's scientific ignorance, when he finally realized that a wonder-flying machine could be built according to the data she gave him; and this made his efforts much easier in convincing his distinguished academic colleagues to take part in the project of building the Jenseitsflugmaschine. He went two steps further and compared Maria's data with Viktor Schauberger and Karl Haushofer data, and to his astonishment, he found out that:

a-Maria' data was scientifically valid,
b-The data of Haushofer and Schauberger were not as developed and progressive as her data.

*** *** ***

229

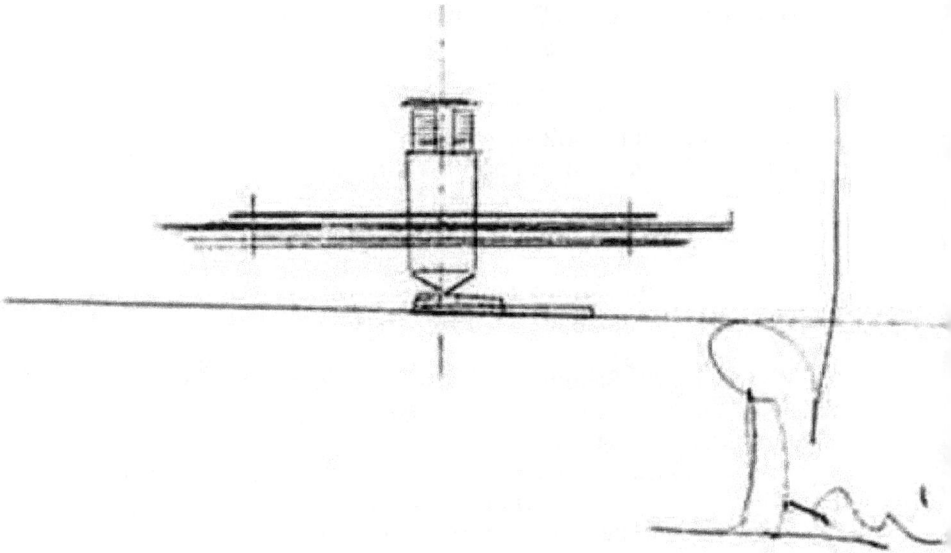

Viktor Schauberger's Jenseitsflugmaschine (JFM).any believe
Schauberger's machine was a replica of Orsic's UFO.

Finally in March of 1922 in Munich, the first secret prototype of
Aldebaran's Jenseitsflugmaschine (Otherworld flight machine;
After-Life Flying Machine) saw the light.
It looked impressive and "Out of this world". But nobody was
hundred per cent sure if this thing could really fly, for first, its
design was so strange, bizarre and unconventional, and second,
making a machine fly without a combustion engine seemed
irrational. A flight-test was scheduled for March 23, 1922.

March 23, 1922: The first flight-test of Aldebaran's Jenseitsflugmaschine

A fiasco!
It was a total failure as many have expected. A gigantic fiasco!
Eye witnesses' reports indicated that the machine blew up after spinning and spinning like fireworks, and the upper layer (Top of the machine) disintegrated, and the lower part (The third level) defragmented like a hand-grenade. Those were the actual words ("disintegrated", "defragmented") used by some of the builders of the Jenseitsflugmaschine.

Dr. Schumann was devastated, but Maria never gave hope.
They went back to the drawing board, and began laboriously to reexamine their data. But all their efforts remained in vain. And by now everybody was convinced that it was a crazy idea! Until, three days later, when Maria Orsic rushed to Dr. Schumann's office with an apparent solution.
She provided him with "Guidance" she claimed she just received from the extraterrestrials.
Dr. Schumann sent her back home, and politely said, "Maria, it was a very exciting project, but gravity is much stronger than any idea I came across. Please go home and forget the whole thing."
Maria Orsic did not argue with him, instead she handed him a few sketches and a series of formulae...and left with a big smile.

Yes, it can be done!
It took Dr. Schumann only two hours to change his mind, "I thought it was useless until I saw something unusual in Maria's drawings...(We don't know what he saw in the new sketches) and then I realized that yes, it can be done..." said Schumann.-From Dr. Professor Winfried Otto Schumann's diary/notes.
Upon hearing the news from Dr. Schumann, Maria was relieved, and for the sake of argument she asked him why did he change his mind?

We don't know what he said.

However we do know that Maria suggested to him to focus his attention on the "Space-time electromagnetic forces"; another concept totally unknown back then.

Dr. Schumann could have not solved the problem without Maria's help!

Mental command and channeling:

My personal opinion is that Dr. Schumann did not solve the problem in its entirety without the help of Maria Orsic, for we know for sure that Maria Orsic brought up the subjects of:

a-Stargates,

b-The 33.33 degree line,

c-Space-time electromagnetic forces,

d-The mental command of the spaceship.

These four items, Professor Schumann was not familiar with, and especially the "Mental Command" of the ship.

By mental command, Maria meant channeling. And I can guess what the reaction of Dr. Schumann was when he heard Maria Orsic talking about MENTAL COMMAND and CHANNELING!!

In fact, the mental command was of a metaphysico-scientific nature based upon very sophisticated aliens' technology, and which consisted of a magnetic band attached to the forehead of Maria which would allow her to command the craft at distance.

Headband Mental Command Device:

Maria explained to Dr. Schumann that the Jenseitsflugmaschine failed to perform as expected because it did not have her mental command. Dr. Schumann went ape, and threatened to quit.

But once again, he changed his mind when Maria Orsic gave him instructions on how to design and build the "Headband Mental Command Device".

It was one surprise after another, but he finally complied with Maria's request.

To many of us, this headband thing seems far fetched, a sort of hallucination in the mind of Maria, but it did materialize, and one set was built.

In fact, a similar headband was retrieved from the debris of a crashed UFO near Roswell in 1947 by the United States Air Force, and was sent to General Arthur Trudeau, then, head of the Foreign Technology Desk at the United States Army's Research and Development Department.

General Trudeau, the father of the reverse engineering of alien technology program.

General Arthur Trudeau was fascinated by the aliens' gadget and right away, he solicited the help of two scientists to unlock its mystery, and thus, the reverse engineering of alien technology program began.
Later on General Carl "Tooey" Spaatz became heavily involved with the program.
This is an absolute fact, no question about it!!!
The "Aliens Transcripts of 1947 and 1948" show beyond the shadow of a doubt that the UFO which crashed near Roswell was mentally commanded from and by a metallic (Unknown alloy) band attached to the skull of the aliens, and their suits which were "glued" to their skin, as part of their bodies were also "animated" by the headband.
The spacecraft of the aliens had no apparent navigation devices and/or dashboards.
The aliens' headband became a major part of the military's alien reverse engineering research/program. The very same headband, Maria Orsic talked about!

A new spaceship is built.
December 17 of 1923: A new model of the super Aldebaran's Jenseitsflugmaschine came to life.

Rebuilding a new spacecraft from scratch was not an easy task.
New material was needed, and it was hard to find. Besides, it was time consuming, and some of the major investors/financiers of the project lost interest, and insufficient funds became a major obstacle, at least in the first stage of rebuilding a new spaceship.
Maria and Ladies of Vril were penniless; money did not mean a thing to them. Maria Orsic earned very little by teaching ballet to beginners and foreign languages to wealthy children.
Her mediumship-channeling séances and services to others were free of charge.

And being the oldest in the Society and the leader of her movement, Maria was responsible for the daily expenses of the Vril-Gesellschaft, as well as the welfare of its members.

It was hard time for everybody, except for the wealthy members of Thule and DHvSS who have invested very heavily in the first ill-fated project. Luckily, they did not mind to refinance the new project from A to Z.

And thus, by December 17 of 1923, a new model of the super Jenseitsflugmaschine came to life. And the big day arrived; the day of the second flight-test of the spaceship.

Is it going to fly?

Maria was absolutely confident, but not everybody in the group shared her enthusiasm.

Nota Bene:

Before, during and after the Jenseitsflugmaschine's successful test-flight, Maria and Sigrun made eight consecutive visits to the hangar where the machine was built, and gave their input and channeling findings to the engineers, especially during the initial stage of construction and the channeled flight-test.

Overseeing the construction of the Jenseitsflugmaschine was not the only reason behind Maria and Sigrun frequent visits to the construction site; they needed to become familiar with the facility, in and out, for one day, Maria and the Ladies of Vril will seize this super flying machine and fly to the stargate of the 33 degree line, where she will rendezvous with the mother-ship of her friends from Adelbaran.

I tend to believe that Dr. Schumann was aware of that fact, but did not say a word to his colleagues.

Why?

I don't know. It is a mystery to me!

Dr. Schumann was a delightful human being, and had lots of respect and admiration for Maria.

He knew she was an extraordinary woman with high ethical standards, and one of a kind. Maria's farewell to Dr. Schumann showed how much they cared for each other.

January, 1924: The first successful flight of Adelbaran's Jenseitsflugmaschine

Note: Read full report on the Jenseitsflugmaschine in my book "GERMAN UFOs: Models & Categories, Engineers & Scientists, Extraterrestrial Messages, Supernatural, Ladies of the Vril, U.S. Link

Sigrun

It was a very successful and a spectacular test-flight. The spacecraft flew at a speed of 300,000 km/hour.

But the Jenseitsflugmaschine landed after fifty five minutes as an archaic machine, looking like a young girl who suddenly has aged 100 years. Maria explained this anomaly by referring to what she called "Parallel Zones". According to Maria, when an object enters a different dimension, its properties are instantly modified, and in some instances totally altered. And this applies to humans too.

The damaged Jenseitsflugmaschine terrified all the engineers, but understandably not Dr. Schumann, because by now, he could tap into the inexplicable metaphysical world of Maria Orsic, and understand the occultic-metaphysical aspect of the project.

Maria: "I am not interested in bombing people and cities."

Worth mentioning that Maria's technical data was used to build other types of UFOs; the most noted one was Vril 7 Geist which was built at Arado-Brandenburg, and flew in 1944. Maria guided the Geist mentally via her channeling abilities; it did not need the headband, Dr. Schumann built for her.

In March of 1944, the engineers who previously worked on the successful Jenseitsflugmaschine asked Sigrun if they could use the Vril Triebwerk in the recently built strategic bomber "E.555", and Sigrun refused categorically.

Maria reacted strongly and said, "I am not interested in bombing people and cities."

Secretly manufacturing two small flying machines

Maria Orsic asked Professor Schumann to tell the members of the Thule and DHvSS that the project needed more work and the flying machine was not perfect yet.

Maria had justifiable reasons; she feared that if the fanatic members from DHvSS and supporters of Hitler discover that the spacecraft in its actual condition could be successfully and immediately deployed, they would not hesitate a second to use it as a destructive war weapon.

Thus, based upon Schumann's recommendations, Maria Orsic's Vril was sent to a hangar in Munich, for further improvements, and consequently, all flights ceased temporarily.

At the same time, Maria and Sigrun were thinking about secretly manufacturing two small flying machines with all the flying properties of the big one, in case, something should happen to it, be confiscated by the authorities, or even stolen.

Maria Orsic's new two circular crafts:
a-OSS records,
b-CIA Helms' files,
c-Statement by Dr. Eugene Sänger,
d-Statement by Major Erich Hartmann,

e-Statement by Lt. Colonel Walter Horten,
f-And of course Professor Shumann's own testimony,
Show that de facto, Maria Orsic's two circular crafts, 27 feet in diameter were produced with the help of four retired engineers.

RFC-2 was one of the two small spacecrafts, designed by Maria, and developed by Dr. Winfried Otto Schumann and four recently recruited engineers. It was elegant, with a shiny metallic surface, made from an unknown alloy; it was this kind of alloy the Russians were extremely interested in, because we know that Stalin's NKVD discussed with Dr. Eugene Sänger how it could be obtained.

RFC-2 was spotted and reported on Sunday 18, March 1945, by Lt. Col. Walter Fellenz, serial number 0-23055 from the United States Army, 42nd Infantry Division, 1st Battalion. The sighting was confirmed by Brigadier General Henning Linden.

To this day, nobody knows the properties of the unprecedented alloy of RFC-2 except -as it was leaked out by NASA insiders in 2007-, by a bunch of engineers and metallurgists working for NASA, and especially on the Shuttle's programs.

Dr. Eugene Sänger

The alloy research program began years ago under the guidance of three German scientists who were recruited by Dr. von Braun for Operation Paperclip, right after the Second World War.

The records show that Dr. Schumann recruited four engineers to develop and build Maria's discs:
- 1-The first was an engineer/architect who previously worked for Messerschmitt's Kokothanki, on the BF 109 G6-14,
- 2-The second was from Focke-Wulf,
- 3-The third was from Heinkel,
- 4-The fourth, from the Bayerische Flugzeugwerke, also known as Bavarian Aircraft Company.

All were carefully and intelligently recruited by Dr. Schumann, because the four scientists had access to material, he desperately needed.

Story confirmed by Major Hartmann:
This story was also confirmed by Major Erich Hartmann when he returned to Germany in October 1955, after spending a 10 year sentence in Russia.
The statements of Major Hartmann appeared in the secret files of Richard Helms (a former CIA director in 1970). Helms kept a voluminous file on Maria Orsic.
In 1945, while serving as the United States intelligence chief in Berlin, Helms obtained vital information on Maria and her Vril spacecraft, yet he kept everything buried in his secret vaults for years.

Major Erich Hartmann died on September 19, 1993 at Weil im Schönbuch. He was considered Germany's greatest fighter ace.
General Dwight Eisenhower admitted that Major Hartmann was the greatest fighter pilot of all times.
Hartmann flew 825 missions and scored 352 victories.
Nota bene:
Professor Schumman did not totally abandon the project.
Records show that he continued with the development of new types and classes of UFOs.

Vril-1-Triebwerk

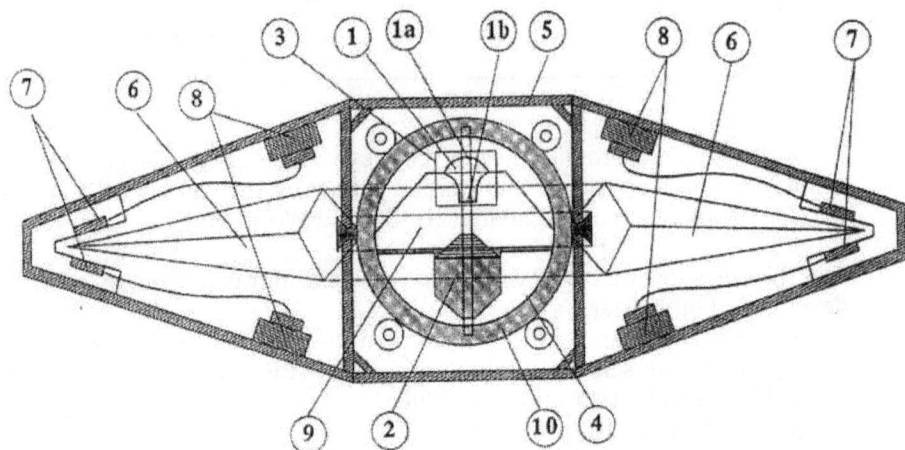

1 Glocke	4 Schwingungseinschluß	10 Schwingungspanzer
1a YX - Pol	5 Rahmen	
1b XY - Pol	6 Drehkörper	
2 Haupt- u. Anlaß	7 Elektromagnete	
Generator	8 Stromspeiser u. Aufnehmer	
3 Glockenmantel	9 Vakuum	

Sketch of the Vril 1-Triebwerk, built upon specifications and
technical data provided by Maria Orsic.

Vril 7 Schnittbild mit Antrieb **Mannschaft**

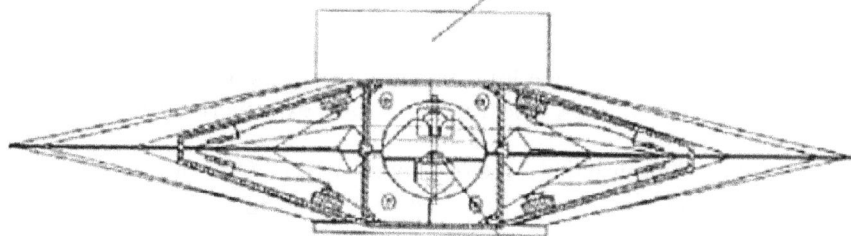

Antrieb

Vril-1-Triebwerk

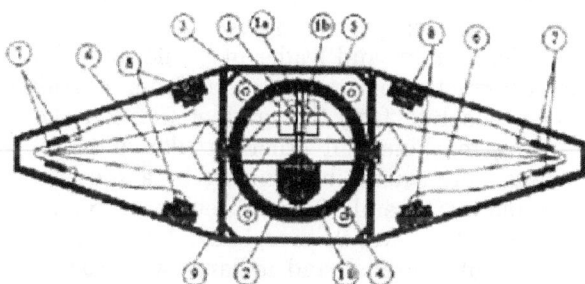

1 Glocke	4 Schwingungseinschluß	10 Schwingungsspanner
1a YX - Pol	5 Rahmen	
1b XY - Pol	6 Drehkörper	
2 Haupt- u. Anlaß	7 Elektromagnete	
Generator	8 Stromspeiser u. Aufnehmer	
3 Glockenmantel	9 Vakuum	

𝕲𝖊𝖒𝖊𝖎𝖓𝖘𝖈𝖍𝖆𝖋𝖙 𝖉𝖊𝖘 𝕾𝖈𝖍𝖜𝖆𝖗𝖟𝖊𝖓 𝕾𝖙𝖊𝖎𝖓𝖘

Rekonstruktionsversuch   **Durchmesser des Geräts ca. 45 m**

Sketch of the Vril 7, built according to Maria's technical data.
Identical data will be used one day, by the Russians to build
their own UFO, which flew twice over Siberia and Leningrad,
and inexplicably vanished from the face of the earth.

American and Russian interests in the Jenseitsflugmaschine:
From 1946 to 1949, the Russians were extremely interested in the
Jenseitsflugmaschine, the German Bell UFOs, and the Nazi extraterrestrials "Super Flying Machines" designed by:

- SS top scientists
- Mediums from "Thule-Gesellschaft"
- Members of the "Thule Society",
- Members of the "Brüder Des Lichts",
- Members from the "Schwarze sonne" and so on.

And of course, Joseph Stalin received numerous reports on Maria Orsic, founder and leader of "Vrilerinnen", the Vril, and her direct contact with extraterrestrials from the Aldebaran.
This is an absolute fact; the original German sketches of the super flying machine and other circular and crescent-shaped flying discs were seized in Germany by a special military task force created by General Dwight Eisenhower, 6 months after the end of World War Two. So everybody, Americans and Russians, British and Poles, French and Italians have heard rumors about Maria Orsic, the German UFOs, and luckily for us, our armed forces in Germany, at the end of the Second World War, put their hands on Germany's secret files on UFO, the RFZ 1 (Rundflugzeug 1), the Horten 229, and several anti-gravity projects carried by Germany's top scientists.
This is documented in:
a-United States naval intelligence files;
b-OSS's files (Precursor to CIA);
c-British Secret Service (MI6) files;
d-General Dwight Eisenhower Special Task Force reports.
As soon as the Red Army captured Berlin, the Russians began looking for Germany's top military scientists, and particularly those who worked on Maria's Vril, the V1, V2, and projects related to UFO.
The Red Army captured 657 German scientists and shipped them to Moscow. A few weeks later, they were sent to military bases and laboratories scattered in several Russian cities.

From left to right: Mikhail Gurevich, Artem Mikoyan.

The secret files of the United States military intelligence during 1945 and early 1946 revealed that:

a-15 German scientists died before they began to work on any project related to UFO and similar programs;

b-345 German scientists were immediately deployed in secret locations;

c-32 German scientists were smuggled outside Russia (To Austria and Switzerland) by Allied forces secret agents and spies, and some ended in the United States and Great Britain;

d-100 German scientists became leading figures in the Russian space programs, avionics, weapons systems, and instrumental in numerous space and rockets programs under the leadership of eminent Russian scientists and engineers like:
a-Artem Mikoyan
b-Mikhail Gurevich
c-Sputnik's Sergei Korolev
d-Sergey Aleksandrovich Afanasyev
e-Mikhail Tikhonravov
Worth mentioning here that Prof. Robert Dopel, Andrei Sakharov, and Igor Kurchatov played an instrumental role in the Russian early study and research of alien reverse engineering.

Andrei Sakharov and Igor Kurchatov.

From left to right: Mikhail Tikhonravov, Sergei Korolev,
pausing in front of Konstantin Tsiolkovsky.

Published by
Times Square Press
New York, Berlin
Website: www.timessquarepress.com

Printed in the
United States of America and Germany
2014